Stepping Into the New Reality

Booklocker.com, Inc.
2008

Stepping Into the New Reality

Karen Bishop

Also by Karen Bishop

Remembering Your Soul Purpose: A Part of Ascension

The Ascension Primer

The Ascension Companion

Staying In Alignment

Table of Contents

Foreword...vii

Questions & Answers Guideline...xiii

Introduction..1

The Broad Ascension Picture..5

How We Evolve and Expand...25

Where We Are Headed...53

Keys To Living In The New Energies 67

Keys of Being: the Feminine 77
　　Shifting Into A New Way Of Being And Thinking............80
　　We Always Have Everything We Need 93
　　Accessing the Higher Realms Through the Earth.............104
　　Not Taking Things Personally 113
　　Creating in the Higher Realms.....................................123
　　Focus and Clarity 162
　　Living Effortlessly With No Struggle or Suffering............171
　　Shutting The Door Behind Us.......................................190

Stepping Stones on Our Path: the Masculine 211
  Knowing Who We Are 214
  Defining Our Path 228
  Connecting With Our Soul Teams and New
    Communities 231
  Identifying Our Geographical Home on Earth 253
  Living Without the Need for Money 266
  Setting Up Our Store-Fronts 279
  Knowing Our Path of Service 289
  Connecting With the Star Beings 296
  Finding Our Heaven 310

Staying In Our Heaven 315

About the Author 325

Foreword

I feel so blessed to be offering this new book, *Stepping Into the New Reality* at this time. As we continue ever onward with our spiritual evolutionary process, or as some say "ascension" process, we continue to arrive in new territory with ever so many surprises, epiphanies, and certainly new challenges to face.

Because the entire planet and all her inhabitants are participating in this experience of expansion and journeying home, many are at varying levels and different phases of their journeys. Some are the fore-runners and way-showers, forging ahead and embodying within themselves new territory and new ways of being, while others are recently expanding and realizing that something vast, holy, and perhaps overwhelmingly confusing is indeed occurring.

Each and every one of us is precisely where we need to be. Before birth, we planned with open hearts and souls how we would each contribute to this process, and where we would place ourselves and our own special energy along the ascension path. Some agreed to begin the process, to thus experience these strange and confusing aspects of the ascension process long before the masses. These brave souls were the first to shake-up the waters and to create an opening for many to follow. Others agreed to hold the space for subsequent levels and layers, at differing rungs and phases of this one-of-a-kind Shift of the Ages. In this way, we are all equally valued and important as we support, create, and bring forth a very New Planet Earth.

Stepping Into the New Reality is thus structured so that you may find yourself in its pages, no matter where you are on your path. Some may say, "Been there, done that, but now I know how far I've come." Or perhaps, "I haven't had that experience yet, but I will know it when I see it!" Or even, "So *that* is what was happening for me!" And maybe you will not relate to this material at all. In this case, this book may not be for you, as it is not for everyone. You will then have the choice to disregard its' content and look elsewhere for material which is more aligned with where you are, or you may simply want to extract the things which ring true for you, and disregard the rest for a later time.

This book is broken into various escalating stages so that you may understand and integrate the material in the best and easiest way possible. After some of the more complex concepts are explained in depth, a much shorter version follows and then a shortest version, to better assist you in gaining more clarity. The higher we evolve, the more we crave simplicity and a very direct interaction, and thus, long passages of complicated text may not suit all of us all of the time. Immediately following other subjects, a brief <u>synopsis</u> of how to stay in alignment with each subject area is described, as an assist in summarizing these concepts. And yet in the concluding sections, different rungs of the ascension ladder are discussed within each section so that you may find yourself now or at least know where you are headed. Whatever the format at any particular time, this book was created with you in mind.

You will find that certain concepts are referred to again and again. Although at times redundant, these concepts are the nuts and bolts of the ascension process, and thus, are an integral part of most all of the information presented here. You may get tired of reading about them, but you will not forget them!

\#Synopsis = a brief, general overview or condensation; summary

Stepping Into the New Reality is an interactive book. It is interactive because you have the opportunity to ask questions along the way. If there are sections that may seem confusing to you, or that may indeed bring up questions, you may very well find the answers in other sections of this book. In this regard, I encourage you to read the entire book before e-mailing a question, but please feel free to ask the questions which tug at you and to which you would truly like some clarity.

The most commonly asked questions will be posted on the *What's Up On Planet Earth?* web site at http://whatsuponplanetearth.com. If your question is selected, you will receive an answer via e-mail along with a posting of your question and its' answer on the web site. You will find the guidelines for asking questions on the *Questions and Answers* page immediately following this one.

The material within this book comes solely from my own personal experiences, from my travels to other dimensions, and from my connection to my soul. It does not contain any channeled material (as I am not a channeler), material from others, or information which I have not personally experienced through my own bumbling and stumbling along the path. If it resembles any material from other sources, I am absolutely thrilled, as this means that many of us are on the same page, and thus, must be onto something valid, important and very real!

Although at times I am able to walk a lot of the information within these pages, as well as finding these principles to be very valid and affirming of higher ways of being and living, I am certainly not at a point where I can embody *all* of these principals 100% of the time. Through trial and error, suffering and awareness, and through visions and openings, my own journey continues ever onward, as I know yours does as well. These ways of being will eventually be embodied by most all of us, but we are, as always, still in transition and still evolving in slow, steady steps. In this way, we eventually get the hang of, completely embody, and have success with one way of being, while we continue to see-saw up and down with others until we eventually embody them completely.

May this book serve as a guideline and light your path as it hopefully serves to simply validate what you already know and are already experiencing.

Wishing you Heaven in your heart, starlight in your soul, and miracles in your life,

Karen

Questions & Answers Guideline

Stepping Into the New Reality gives you the opportunity to ask questions about the book content and/or how it may relate to situations you may be experiencing in your life.

Although I am unable to answer all of the questions I receive, I look forward to reading each and every one. The most frequently asked questions will be posted on the *Questions & Answers* page on the *What's Up On Planet Earth?* web site at http://www.whatsuponplanetearth.com. If your question is not selected, there is a good chance you will find a very similar one, along with its' answer, among the many listed there...someone else asked it for you!

The *Questions & Answers* page has been created to connect us through knowing that we are all one at our core, and thus, having the same experiences. I welcome you in checking this page as often as you like, as it will be updated frequently. The questions and answers are arranged by category so that you may find with ease, the subject matter that is currently the most prevalent to you.

If your question is selected, you will receive an answer via e-mail, along with its' posting on the web site.

To ask a question, please email your question to:

steppingquestions@whatsuponplanetearth.com

Kindly be as brief as possible (one or two short paragraphs or less...a few sentences preferred), and include your email address for a response if it is different from the one you are sending from. Your email address will not be shared with anyone and will not be posted on the web site. In addition, only your initials will be used in order to ensure your privacy.

Many have asked over the years that I include a community section on the web site so that individuals can connect to one another. For various reasons, I have chosen not to provide this service.

Happy reading! I look forward to hearing from you!

Introduction

One day while out hiking in a vast expanse of nature where I was then living in the mountains of Northeastern Arizona, I jumped more fully into the higher realms...or into a higher dimension and way of living and being.

Even though we may go in and out of higher knowledge and higher vibrating ways of being at times in a sporadic way, or perhaps during an energy shift, everything was all so very clear that day, and completely in its' entirety in a permanent and all-encompassing way. Yes, this particular day, it was all there in one big and wonderful piece, with all the dots connected. While being totally in a new reality, much was right before my eyes and so very evident. It was not a piece here and a piece there, but the entire pie. And I was in it with all my senses, blessed to be experiencing this higher dimensional reality with all my being while still in the physical.

The most evident awareness I had while in this reality was the simple fact that much of all that we have created thus far has simply been one, big, enormous illusion. We created it from limited thinking and from the perspective of our own lower vibrating filters. The new reality was always there...right over our heads...but we simply were not completely focused there or able to actually and easily reside there...*until now.*

Why now? Why are we suddenly, and more importantly, *finally* poised to begin living and being in a higher dimensional reality?

Because we are now vibrating higher individually and as a whole, as a direct result of our on-going ascension or spiritual evolutionary process.

So in a way, we could say that we have actually earned it. We have stretched, moaned, groaned, let go, purified, released lower vibrational energy, and re-aligned more fully with the higher realms. "Earning it," then, means matching a higher level of vibration in order to access it. We can always drop into lower vibrating realities and dimensions for short periods of time, but we cannot access higher vibrating dimensions or become aware and really "see" and fully understand their ways of living and being, until we are vibrating the same within ourselves. This is what opens the gate and grants our access. We now get to receive the fruits of our expansion and evolutionary process as we continue to arrive in one new phase or dimensional level after another. So then, each new phase or new reality more fully matches the very new and higher vibration which we now embody. *And we are taking the entire planet with us.*

There were several key concepts that became evident while I viewed and experienced this new reality. These concepts continue to become a part of my everyday life, and I know they are becoming a part of yours as well, as we continue our on-going process of spiritual expansion. These are concepts that reflect key components of living in a higher dimension, or a new reality. And they are wonderfully exciting and incredibly awesome indeed... because once we begin to utilize them, we will automatically and magically be placed in alignment with the new higher vibrating energies that are now more present than ever before.

It is these concepts that will be highlighted and light your way as you begin your journey through the pages of *Stepping Into the New Reality*.

Please join me as I take you step-by-step into a very new reality in the higher realms. May you enjoy your journey as much as I am enjoying mine...

~The Broad Ascension Picture ~

What Exactly Is Ascension and Who Cares?

A **more all** encompassing and fully detailed description of our spiritual evolutionary or ascension process can be found in the book *The Ascension Primer* (available at http://www.whatsuponplanetearth.com), but for our purposes here, a general description is required to help with the understanding and integration of the information in this book. Hence, a general background is as follows:

Our current universe has experienced all that it has chosen to and gone as far as it can go. A group of souls (commonly referred to as "lightworkers," and if you are reading this material and resonating deeply with it, you are most likely one of these souls), created the current universe where we reside. It was a game...something to do with energy, something to occupy our time so to speak. We created what we refer to as "God" for this particular universe and we created a house or playground so that we could experience and create with energy while in form....and this we call our universe.

Several of us split off from the spark of the Creator, or Original God, at the same time, and in this regard, we are all soul mates. Because we created ourselves at about the same time, we have a very special connection. This very special connection stems from the fact that we share the same energy. The vibration at the time of our creation was the same, so then, we vibrate very similarly. This is why I am able to write the energy alerts (kindly visit http://www.whatsuponplanetearth.com to access these regularly posted energy alerts free of charge), and why so many of us can relate to the information contained in them, as we are all one and vibrating similarly at our core. We are like the roots of an enormous aspen tree grove, being sustained by and sharing the same energy stream. And being that we were created at about the same time, we then share more similar energy than most...and most certainly, currently a very similar general purpose...that of creating and experiencing in form, the Shift of the Ages. Our shared purpose of evolving energy through the house of ourselves creates, as well, the phenomenon of experiencing and feeling the same things at the same time.

So then, we created this universe to experience energy so that we could create whatever our minds and spirits could envision. This is called life. This is about energy utilizing form. It was intended to be fun and ever joyful. Our experiences here were never intended as "lessons" with a goal to return to a higher vibrating version of ourselves. This concept developed from the limited 3D mind of mis-perceptions...mis-perceptions of darkness and struggling. We came to simply experience....period. As things evolved, we eventually realized that we had gone as far as we could, experienced all that we wanted to, and decided to wrap things up, cash in all of our chips, and call it a day. Thus, the Shift of the Ages was hatched and ready to be birthed.

With this finalizing next step agreed upon, we then infused our energy into form so that we could "ascend," or expand ourselves back to the beginning, while in the physical. And thus, we all came together into physical forms for this very exciting purpose. (But we are really expanding all of the universe as a whole. We are so evolved at our soul levels, that we knew we could accomplish this, and joyfully agreed to, as a service to ourselves and all of the creations in the universe. After all, we originally created it all, and *were* it all, so as we "expand," we are really just re-capturing everything that currently exists, which originated from us anyway. Phew!)

As the original creators of the planet Earth, we were most entitled to be a part of the finalizing step... we wanted to finish what we had originally begun. This last step would enable all life in the universe to follow our lead. It would enable every existing life form to come after us, as each and every representative of living energy in some type of form would be affected, in every far reaching corner of the universe...we would therefore be bringing everything in the universe along with us, as we evolved back into the purest form of life where we initially began. *This is a journey of returning home.*

We decided that this amazing and pivotal event would take place on the planet Earth. So in this way, all eyes are upon us, as we are so highly revered and watched over as we go through this monumental process, even though at times we may feel very inadequate, insecure, and not remember who we are. And know that all higher vibrating non-physical beings are really just aspects of ourselves as well. As we continue with our evolutionary process, shedding off all the lower vibrating aspects for the whole (the whole being other aspects of ourselves as well), we then slowly begin to re-unite with these higher vibrating aspects as we become more of them ourselves...not for the first time, but as a closer vibrating match right now, as we evolve in our current form. When we are complete with spinning off and shedding all the aspects of ourselves where we had infused our energy (embodying the entire universe at one time or another), for eons of time since our first original spark of origin, we will then leave this planet Earth in its' original pristine condition, and retire. Are you still awake, as you read this complicated scenario (it can be difficult to describe!)?

In this way, we are all one.

Retire to where? When we are done with our experience in this universe, where do we go? Is it really *the end*?

I remember a time when I was giving a soul reading to a woman who had come to visit me. Wanting some answers for herself, as she was in a transitional period (when are we not?), I had decided to take a peek. As always, all was in perfect order, even though it had appeared otherwise. But the most exciting part of the reading, was seeing her soul, its' history, and where it would be heading from here. And she was a truly ancient soul indeed, as many of us are.

This was when I first found myself truly blessed to "see" the end of the plan. There through the dimensions were layers of universes, each one vibrating higher than the next...and they went on for infinity. I could see that when she was complete with her voluntary assignment and experience of taking part in our ascension process, through herself, she would be "graduating" in vibration and soul experience to a very new and much higher universe where none of us currently here have yet resided.

When we are finished purifying, releasing, and in this way, assisting all life to do the same, as we volunteered to do it through ourselves (because at some point we were all every creation), we will have completed what we have begun. We will then have left a very new and pristine planet Earth for all the new arrivals who wish to experience creating in form. We will be done with this universe. We will be complete.

The Proof Is In The Pudding

"How in the world do you know this, Karen?" you might be wondering. "Why should I believe you? This sounds like a crazy story from a wild imagination."

Well... you really shouldn't believe me. Our own personal realities are only comprised of our beliefs. So all we can really do is to connect with what resonates within us, and throw out the rest. No one is ever really "right" or "wrong."

I have found that what works best for me, is to expand my awareness through personal experience and through my travels to the higher dimensions. Like others on the planet, I was born wide open and able to remember and "see" other dimensions and realities...and this is what has been my navigator since birth. I am not a channeler, as I do not receive information from higher beings or from a higher Source. For me, I "go there" myself and experience it myself. So then, I have found that my personal adventures and experiences are what work for me in order to expand. Not through the writings of others, or through the messages from any non-physical beings, or even through the experiences of others, as we always see things and perceive things through our own individual filters. And cloudy perceptions will be the way we "see," until we purify ourselves to a great degree. Our own personal experiences then, are great navigators to higher ways of living and being.

When we simply receive information from another, if even from a higher vibrating non-physical being, it can really have no meaning for us until we actually experience it or "see" it ourselves. Basically, much of everything is simply moot until we go through it ourselves. (Even though the non-physicals can certainly be great at validating and explaining our experiences, or even as wonderful companions.)

And this is why the ascension process is so very amazing. We are truly living it. This is also why the non-physical beings that vibrate the highest, have backed off. They know that this is our deal, and that it comes from our own experience and from choice. Remember, we were the original creators of all of life, we infused ourselves into the reality of our creations, and it is now, then, our role to bring it all to completion. And this is why what I write only comes from my own personal experience, along with my connection to my soul and to Source, along with this amazing and awe inspiring ascension process. It is only meant to serve as a validation of all our experiences, as we are all one.

So what "proof" do we have that any of this wild tale may be accurate at all? And do we even really need any proof?

Have you felt in recent years and months, that you were stretching far beyond what you had the capacity to endure? Have you had many emotional ups and downs, strange physical aches and pains, many losses in the form of friends, jobs, family, finances, and much of anything else? Have you had strange sleeping disturbances, dizziness, neck and back pain, an intolerance for lower vibrating energy, and abdominal weight gain, bloating, or weight loss? Do you wonder who you are looking at in the mirror? Is it hard to remember and identify with the childhood version of you? Have you had a serious medical situation that left you feeling helpless and powerless? Do you often feel spaced out with no sense of place? Are your emotions out of control from time to time? Do you have trouble remembering the smallest of things? Do you ever feel lost and alone? Do you at times feel that there is nowhere left to go that remotely fits you anymore? Do you have a strong sense that you are here to accomplish something, but you cannot remember what it is? Do you "miss" something, but are not sure exactly what?

If you have experienced any of the above, you are most likely having the most common of the ascension symptoms and experiences. There are far too many to list here, and far too many of us having these strange and common occurrences to warrant them as an accident or perhaps some kind of bizarre virus. These symptoms and experiences are a direct result of our spiritual expansion process, as we begin to vibrate higher and to embody more light than ever before. (A brief note: It is always best to seek medical attention when necessary, as certainly not all of our strange symptoms can be attributed to the ascension process.)

Have you felt very tired since the year 2000? Do you ever feel done in, or simply feel that you don't care much anymore? Do you ever feel as though there is nothing much left to do, or perhaps that there is no more learning for you on the horizon? Have you quit reading spiritual and personal growth material? Are you ready to retire? Tired of "teaching" and bringing up the vibration of the planet? Are you ready to go out to pasture and smell the roses? Is it hard for you to imagine what could possibly be next? Do you want to go back "home"?

If you have had any of the feelings in the previous paragraph, it is most likely because you are nearly done here with your experience. You have experienced it all and there is nowhere left to go in this particular universe. The only thing left, then, is to prepare this universe for the new arrivals through the ascension process on planet Earth. And the exciting news is that a very new experience, with things that we have never known or experienced before, is on the very next horizon, in the very next universe. And.... we get to arrive there with our beloved brothers and sisters....all as one. There are really no words to describe what this looks like, as it is so difficult to even wrap a human mind around. It is truly an awesome feeling of unity, completion, and an incredible energetic event, when viewed from a higher dimension.

There are those who may not feel this sense of completion. These souls are here for subsequent phases that follow the departure or retirement of the light bearers who started the whole thing. Each and every one of us is right where we need to be. These souls may indeed feel very excited about their new endeavors and have a strong longing to stay here and be a large part of the New World. And the New World will be developed with no interference and no more of the common ascension experiences and phases of readiness we are accustomed to, once we reach 2012 and beyond. The original creators of the planet will then have a choice to stay and experience their versions of Heaven on Earth, be a part of creating the New World, or move on to the next universe. They will have earned their gold watches and their rightful choices (these are notably baby boomers, but there are always exceptions as well).

When 2012 arrives, many of us will feel a dramatic sense of "done." It will signal the next phase and the arrival of the New World. For those of us who are highly sensitive and tapped in, the arrival of 2012 will feel dramatically intense, as if everything is indeed over....an internal switch will be activated. These feelings are occurring now for some, but to a much smaller degree as we are heading for the completion of this monumental cycle in small incremental steps. So then, the world will not suddenly end, as it has been ending for awhile now in small but important and necessary steps. In 2012, the New World will finally *arrive*. It will be a strange time indeed, but we will have arrived at this place in gradual evolutionary steps, so it will be much more of a beginning than an end....all culminating in one prefect place ready for a very new creation. The advent of 2012 will simply be a signal with the support of corresponding energies of the cosmos and planets, that we have reached another pivotal point. 2012 is then, not all of it. It is simply a pivotal piece in a vast game of beginning the universe all over again.

When we made a dramatic shift as a whole in the year 2008, much of the entire planet was embraced. Until then, individual souls experienced their ascension process at varying times, with a few leading the way while more and more were embraced as time went on. This pattern, will of course, continue on for quite awhile. But after an impressive critical mass was reached in 2008, the new souls, or new babies began arriving. These very new souls are creating a high vibrating grid which will serve to cement in or lay a very dynamic foundation for the New World, which will come forth very pristinely in 2012 and beyond. These new souls are coming in droves. After we experienced this awesome shift in 2008, they knew it was time, and the flood gates opened. There was an epidemic of twins, premature births, and the like as so many were ready to be here for the times to come. They needed to hold the higher energy as well, in order for the planet to remain intact while it began in earnest the most intense phase of "the fall."

These new babies are very powerful indeed. They know exactly who they are, why they are here, what they want, and will accept nothing less. They are strong leaders and will be unswayed in what they are here to create. Nothing will be able to affect them. They are so very sure of themselves as they have such a distinct mission. They know what the New World looks like and are here to make it happen. True creators they are indeed, as they are not here to make change, shake things up, or bring in a higher vibration, so to speak. They are here to create, pure and simple, while they oh so naturally carry a higher vibration within themselves.

The new souls which began arriving around 2008 are indeed "new." Thus, they are not souls which embody aspects of ourselves which we need to release or spin off. These souls are the beginning of the new. And it is these souls who will begin the very New World while many of us get to retire, or simply choose to stay and experience our Heaven on Earth.

Many of you reading this material are already vibrating as high as these new babies, and because of this, will love to be in their company. With so much of the old still vibrating lower than the forerunners of the ascension process, being in the company of a vibration equal to our own can make us feel very at home and at peace, while much of the rest of the planet can feel downright uncomfortable at best. But we will eventually vibrate or evolve beyond even these new little ones. There will be a new wave of births around 2012 as well.....and these babies will be another breed entirely!

So then, for us "old folks" or old souls who are still remaining, our vibration in form will eventually be too high for this universe and we will then be granted access to the next one through the law of vibrational hierarchies. (Actually, our vibration at our soul levels is already high enough now, but we are completing what we began before we can move on.....*and*, preparing it for the very new inhabitants.) Again, we will eventually be vibrating higher than the new babies, and many of us already are. Yes, we will have earned our admittance to this new land (or very new universe) indeed. And we need not fret about our remaining days here on Earth, as we will come to finally experience the Heaven on Earth that we have always known was possible. Again, it is precisely then that we can choose to leave, or stay as the beautiful and loving angels of the Earth that we will eventually become.

"You are freaking me out Karen," some of you may be thinking. "I am feeling as though I will be leaving everything behind and it feels downright scary and uncomfortable. I don't want to go anywhere." When we come to this place, it will not feel this way. We will have many choices, as we are now vibrating so high. We will be able to visit our loved ones as often as we choose, we will be taking many of them with us, and when we are at this level, we will no longer have the same lower vibrating emotions that we have now. All will, as always, be in divine and perfect order. We will have with us our most beloved companions with whom we have shared experiences for eons of time. We will actually be re-united as a whole. It will be one glorious reunion like no other. I promise!

So understanding and knowing that we are evolving very rapidly through an ascension process might matter in that this knowledge can bring us peace of mind, acceptance, and even at some point, gratitude for this one-of-a-kind, amazing occurrence. Knowing that we are evolving can also allow us to know that all is really in divine and perfect order. And yes, there is a plan....and it is a higher level plan. And the best part is that we are the ones who are planning it!

It is my greatest desire that this book rekindle within you what you have always known, and that it serves to re-connect you with the deepest aspects of your soul. Do you remember our plan? Do you remember who you are and why you are here? Ahhhh...the beauty of our souls!

- -

A shorter version:

The universe is ending, winding up, and collecting everything it experienced so far, in readiness to begin again in a more pure and simple form. We are the ones who started and created this experience in the first place, so we are thus the ones who are bringing everything to a close. After we are done, we will then have the choice to continue on in a very new universe that vibrates much higher than any we have experienced thus far, or we may stay here and continue on as angels of the earth.

Others who come after us, will stay here as the very new inhabitants of a very new planet Earth, and it will reside in a dimension we have now evolved out of.

The shortest version:

We are dismantling all the aspects of our souls that we infused into every reality in this universe in readiness to move to another level. Ouch! That sounds harsh!

~ How We Evolve and Expand ~

As I began to evolve into new ways of being, and especially into new ways of living, early in 2007 I found myself ready to move into a new phase. I had embodied a vision of higher ways of living for as long as I can remember, as I am sure many of you reading this have as well.

One pivotal aspect of this vision involved living in total harmony with the earth, and thus utilizing all her bounty, utilizing the gifts that the celestial bodies bring, living in a natural or earthen home (as we ascend through the earth), and most importantly, living in alignment with higher energies as much as possible.

So then, it was finally time to start living in this way. The earth and her inhabitants had reached another plateau as a whole in December of 2006, and it was most assuredly, then, time for the next phase.

Thus began a very new adventure involving spending substantial amounts of time on the ancient sites in the area where I lived in Northeastern Arizona, learning and experiencing their highly connected and very aligned ways of living and being, and receiving exciting information that had yet been unnoticed or not revealed until now. When the energies and vibration of our planet reach a certain level, much is activated, unlocked and revealed, thus opening new sources of higher information for us all. When we reach a new plateau, new doors open for us as well. Through a series of synchronicities and new connections, I was suddenly being handed access to the ancient sites so that their higher ways could be revealed and thus utilized to create the New World. It was an exciting time indeed.

Gaining access to many of these ancient sites involved hiking up steep terrain, as many of them are perched upon ancient rocky cliffs, and some involved a long hike of several miles in order to reach them at all. In this regard, my physical agility, stamina, and strength were soon in for a great test. Maneuvering around large mounds of enormous rocks, accessing ancient fissures, and becoming more like a mountain goat each day seemed to be a new reality that could not be overlooked.

Many years ago, when I experienced my first spiritual awakening, my legs became paralyzed for about a year for no apparent reason. Since that time, and along with having my right leg crushed and rebuilt from an automobile accident in 2001 (another spiritual expansion experience!), I do not have great leg strength. I had tried all kinds of therapy, undergone many healings and treatments to strengthen my legs, but after years of trying, I had finally come to a point where I chose to accept things as they were.

But then an interesting thing happened. Visiting these ancient and most times hidden and secret sites involved having a guide, and because of this, I became connected to a man named Phil. Phil knew of just about every ancient place that existed in my area, as well as having vast amounts of knowledge regarding these ancient cultures and their ways of living and being. Having a background as an EMT (Emergency Medical Technician), he guided us to these sites and within them, in a way that was respectful of my physical limitations, but also in a way that stretched my abilities just enough to create new strength.

It was not long until I suddenly realized that I was easily scaling cliffs and rocky terrain that I would absolutely never have been able to before. In the past, my legs would get so weak that I could not use them for several days after a strenuous hike or even after simply accessing an ancient staircase through a rocky fissure. But by having Phil as my guide, and by respecting and honoring him along with what and how he was guiding me, my leg strength was able to grow in slow and steady ways. Before I knew it and much to my surprise, I had created vast improvement in my legs that I had never experienced in nearly 30 years! And on top of this, it happened without me even consciously trying.

My usual pattern was to move quickly ahead, straight up, and to get to where I was going as fast as possible. When we have a specific soul purpose (mine is to go ahead of the masses and report back), at times we can mistakenly utilize it 24/7 and especially in an over-abundant way if we are running an unusual amount of energy through our vehicles, which most of us are. Learning to utilize our purpose when it is needed and connecting to the whole in a relaxed and enjoyable way the remainder of the time, is a way of being which is continually missed by many of us. By allowing Phil to take the lead through his own expertise, I was blessed to receive an enormous gift and could then turn mine off as it was certainly not needed now. But I must say, I had a challenge at first, as I was so used to going ahead at a rapid speed!

And this is the way of ascension. This is how we evolve and expand...in slow, gradual steps, without trying or intentionally seeking ways to evolve, just as my legs had found out.

Jumping to the highest level first, rarely works. It is much too stressful. Going to the next level which is the easiest and which feels the best, is usually the best thing for us and always the most healthy way to go. This then, is the pattern that the ascension process follows as well. At times we may feel that we are stretched to the maximum, and at other times we may feel that nothing is ever going to change. But this miraculous process of spiritual evolution is always progressing right on schedule.

We expand and grow, reach a new level of vibration, and then wait for everyone else to catch up. It is truly exciting indeed, even though it might not feel like it at times. Even though we may have our visions of what things should look like, and are eager to be there right away, we cannot truly get there until we are actually vibrating in the same way of our vision, and many times until enough of the population has arrived along side of us.

I have jumped ahead and gone far beyond the masses before, and I can tell you, it is very lonely being the only one there! There is nothing much to relate to, we can feel that we have no sense of place, do not belong anywhere, and have no one to interact with that understands or is experiencing things the way we now are. The ascension process is challenging in this way in its own time, so pushing things can really make this process much more challenging. The universe, our souls, and our loving non-physical guardians know exactly what they are doing. And innately, I truly believe that we want everyone else there with us. We are one at our core, and know that we belong with our brothers and sisters. In addition, those referred to as "lightworkers" are programmed to take everyone with them...it is part of the plan.

So then, energy builds (the pain and pressure!), is integrated (this is the ouchy part!), we wait (this is the frustrating part!), and then we move forward into higher vibrating creations and a higher vibrating reality (this is the glorious part, but we never get to be here for long!). It is all about stepping stones, stepping stones, stepping stones. We cannot create a higher vision until we are truly vibrating and being this vision ourselves. We must match it in all ways before it can manifest in all ways. Jumping ahead can be truly stressful and it can also make us feel as though we have gone insane. The ascension process makes us feel we have lost our minds anyway. Why add to this traumatic scenario?

When we are truly *being* the next step, then we are in alignment with it, and it will manifest for us effortlessly. Gaining leg strength in a way that was slow and steady, allowed me to fully utilize the ultimate power of my legs, and in a totally natural way. Receiving healings, activations, or meddling , intrusive, artificial alignments only serves to force the process, just as too much trying and physical therapy had done for my legs. When things just *fit* where we are right now, then we are in the perfect energy for manifesting and for change. And this is how evolution works. This is why it is unusually difficult to create any far out magnificent visions that are not in alignment with where we currently are. It is always easiest to begin with where we are now and follow the stepping stones to these higher visions.

One way that the entire planet could suddenly look like many of us might wish to envision it, would be if huge natural disasters occurred, or if we were hit by a large comet, or perhaps if we experienced some great and all-encompassing plague. These scenarios might clear out the denser energy in one big and sudden whoosh! But at our highest soul levels, we are planning the best scenario, and we always plan things according to choice at the time, how things are progressing, and what would be beneficial to the most. Many individuals are still experiencing growth while on the earth, have a desire to be here for part of this amazing ascension experience, and are not ready to depart quite yet. They can still benefit from their residency here, so a sudden and extreme evolutionary scenario is not our best choice. In addition, we are always creating as we go. This is part of the fun...creating this special process of ascension! In this way, there are always surprises as well. Oh, how I love the surprises!

Another example of evolving too quickly would be a third world country that was suddenly liberated from some kind of dictatorship by an outside meddling third party with good intentions. The newly liberated country usually struggles to a great degree, and many times creates a disastrous scenario on their own after they have been liberated. This is because the country is not yet vibrating or *being* what is needed to sustain itself and create a higher level interactive community. They have been forced to leap ahead in their vibration from a meddling "I will save you" third party.

So then, what if an asteroid hit the planet, much was destroyed, and what was left had free reign to create a higher living society and higher ways of being? Are we ready yet? Are enough of us vibrating so high within ourselves that we could create such a thing? I say that we are not yet there. And this is what evolution is about. When enough of us truly match, in all ways, these higher ways of living and being, then the only possible scenario is one that would create on the outside, what is existing inside of us.

This is the way energy works, and this is why much of everything is always in divine, right, and perfect order. We must match our visions by vibrating and *being* them ourselves, before we can create them. Just having them in our "heads" is not enough. We may have been born with these visions and carried them around for a lifetime, but we have to "be" them, walk our talk, and embody them before they can manifest. A monumental task indeed, but we are making enormous progress. When we are simply *being* our visions by embodying them in their totality, we do not need to push, have a great desire for them, or even feel cheated without them. This is because we are already there, and then the wanting ceases....and this is when everything we *used to* desire arrives!

Remember, we can only go from where we are now. We must first balance or let go of any lower vibrating energies within us before we can move forward into a higher dimensional reality. If we try to move forward before we are done with this process (by making a change in our lives, for instance), we would simply create exactly the same scenario that we are trying to escape from.

Staying In Alignment With Each New Stepping Stone

How do we complete our process at one stepping stone before we can then move on to another? *Neutralizing* any lower vibrating energies within us (usually through acceptance and understanding, resulting from defusing any extreme lower vibrating emotions and resistance we may have) is mandatory before we can move forward in a more permanent way. We let go of any lower vibrating energies and we balance any energies that we will be keeping. What did you just say, Karen?

The ascension process serves to bring in higher vibrating energies. They used to arrive more from the outside, resulting from a summoning from the way-showers who had gone ahead (whether consciously or not, depending upon how connected each of us is to our souls...the more connected we are to our souls, the more conscious we are about many high level things that are occurring). "From the outside" meant through solar flares, meteor showers, equinox and planetary alignments, and the like. The higher vibrating energies seemingly arrived all on their own, whether we were ready or not! Thus, in the beginning stages, we may have felt clobbered and as though something was happening "to us" when these higher vibrating energies arrived. We were not as connected to our souls then as we are now, thus, our awareness was more limited.

Over time, the way-showers began to embody more and more light within themselves, and thus started the process of bringing souls (or the rest of the planet) along with them who were at lower rungs of the ascension ladder. Now, so many more individuals are beginning their process, and now embodying more light, that a shift has occurred. Things began to snowball after a while, and thus, the shifts began occurring more from within than without. The shifts now arrive much more often when we reach levels of critical mass, or rather when enough individuals on the planet are carrying and embodying higher light. The more we evolve, the more we operate as a whole.

This is why it may appear that there is more darkness now for longer stretches of time. This is why when a cosmic occurrence arrives, we may feel good for only a short time, and then things seem to dissipate. We are embodying more light now, so *we* are the ones who need to create the shifts and the change, and then align them with the cosmic events that arrive to support us. This is why the waiting also occurs at times before a shift can arrive. We are waiting for enough souls to be ready or to arrive at a certain vibrational frequency within themselves. We want everyone on board.

So then, the energetic shifts are now much more dictated by what is going on *within* us, as we, ourselves, are carrying the light more than ever before. We no longer need so much help from the outside. This is why at times, our progress seems to sputter, and does not seem to really take off....there are not then, enough of the masses at a certain level, so we only move forward an inch at a time. And to add even more confusion to this scenario, a substantial cosmic occurrence will not take place until enough of the masses are ready for its' benefit. We summon from the inside through our vibrational level and readiness, and the outside then responds in kind. Creation always occurs when everything meets in the middle at the very same moment. Things are going slower now, or rather the big surges of light are much less frequent and for shorter amounts of time, because many more are now carrying the light, and much more of it. And again, we are much more of a whole now.

Suppose you had a car that was out of gas (or light). Eventually, you were able to fill up your gas tank, so you started the engine, readying for a big leap forward, onto the highway. But the car would only go forward in small, sputtering stretches, even though your tank was full. You eventually realized that some of the parts in the engine were not functioning to their full capacity, as they were broken and needed tweaking or repair (the masses). After you repaired the engine, and with your full tank of gas that had been waiting for a while now, you were then off to a very new horizon in full throttle.

And we will "repair" the parts of the engine (or the masses), by assisting and serving through our store-fronts. Then we will all go forward one more rung as individuals within the whole.

How, then, do we complete our process at one stepping stone before we can move on to another?

When new energies do arrive, each of us is then given an opportunity to adjust by making changes within ourselves and within our belief systems and perceptions. These changes occur through purging, releasing, or balancing energies within us, and thus...a move forward is created. If we willingly choose to flow with this process, we are able to see more clearly how we have been vibrating (or what we have been mis-perceiving and believing), honor and accept this, and then let it go as we are now ready to vibrate higher. In this way, we can at times wonder who in the world we now are, as so much of us no longer seems to exist! Thus, the continual loss of identity that the ascension process creates.

Ouch! There is also a little twist present as well with this process. The evolutionary process we are experiencing also creates feelings of intolerance and some other fairly unpleasant feelings when in the presence of lower vibrating energies (some of us who are acutely sensitive can feel downright repulsed, not seeming very spiritual!). This is partly because we are being encouraged to move forward and create something new that is of a higher vibration, but it is mostly because higher and lower vibrating energies cannot exist in the same space. There is then, a vast mis-match now present, and it can feel downright uncomfortable at best when we are around these old energies.

So then, after we understand, have love for, and integrate within us these lower vibrating energies in a more balanced way (and in many cases release them altogether), we can then move forward and no longer need to experience or be in their presence again in the same way. And after we are done with this process, it can feel downright awful to be around the density of these old energies that may surround us! So then, it can really be a challenge to accept and have love for energies that we have no tolerance for! Thus, our personal sanctuaries become our individual Heaven until the whole can catch up. But because the whole is almost always at varying levels of the ascension process, there is almost always present a rocky road in this regard. Even though we may wait until enough of the masses are ready, before we experience the substantial shifts, the masses are still on a variety of levels.

How can we experience the intolerance of lower vibrating energies and also love and understand them at the same time? How can we be in their presence for long without feeling so uncomfortable? What a challenge indeed, and this is the way of dimensional hierarchies. Just like the non-physicals and the angels, we can go to lower dimensions, but only for brief periods of time. We can also go higher for very brief periods (during interdimensional travel or while giving a reading, etc.), but the higher we go, the more exhausted we become, as too much of our reserves are utilized . We cannot go higher unless there are at least some aspects of ourselves which are embodying these higher dimensions, thus allowing access to begin with. In regard to the ascension process, we gain permanent access to the higher realms when we are permanently vibrating higher. So then, the ascension process is thus taking the entire planet as a whole into a much higher dimension, step by step.

"This sounds very confusing and complicated to me," you might be thinking. Or perhaps, "I don't feel like concentrating this hard! This sounds like one big confusing mess! How in the world are we supposed to live in this chaos and continual transition?"

Here's a simple guideline to follow for a better understanding of this process: If you are feeling icky and heavy in certain energies, *very tired of them*, feel as though you are drowning, feel frightened, feel as though they have nothing to do with you, and have a strong desire to flee, you have most likely evolved beyond them. If you are feeling angry, resistive, mortified, in great disagreement with, have judgment, and are frustrated with certain energies, it is probably time for you to diffuse these emotions through acceptance and love, as you look within yourself to see what you are embodying that serves to connect you to them.

When we have a deep, painful, sad, and almost gagging reaction to lower vibrating energies (not an emotional, resistive, and personal reaction), can barely relate to them, feel very heavy and suffocated by them, and *have a severe preference to be somewhere else,* then this is because we are residing in a dimension or higher realm where these energies can no longer exist. It can be easy to become entangled in the cop-out that we are more highly evolved than others, and use this as an excuse to disregard what is still inside of us, thus placing blame on another. No leaping, remember? The ascension process is a step-by-step evolutionary process, and it takes a long time.

One day I was at the dump here in my small town, getting rid of some bags of trash. There is a man who works there, whom I had come to interact with during each visit, who is about 6' 6" tall, very hefty, and on oxygen. Frequently I asked him how he was, and at times asked him if he needed more water on hot days, and even a snack or two. During my last visit there, he was standing outside of his shack when I greeted him in my usual exuberant way. That particular hot day in New Mexico, I was wearing a light white top with skimpy straps, a pair of shorts, and some hiking boots. As he walked over to me, he grabbed one of my breasts and made some disrespectful and bizarre comments about them as he laughed and made small talk. Very taken aback and totally confused, I decided that the conversation was over and jumped in my car and drove off.

During my younger years, I had experienced rapes as a toddler, various molestations, and unending attention from men at all ages of my life. Healings did not much affect this energy that I embodied for so many years, but the ascension process did. Very naturally, and without a huge amount of effort, I was finally able to diffuse these experiences and the emotions and reactions they had created within me.

Thus, as I drove away, it felt as though this experience had happened to someone else. It did not remotely trigger anything within me. What I did feel, was a great love, caring, and deep sadness for my "friend" and where we was residing in his unhealthy world. Although surprised and taken aback by his behavior, I could only feel sad for where he was, while having a strong desire to never be in his presence again. Within an hour, it was as if nothing had ever happened. I soon found a very new place to deposit my trash in the pueblo of Zuni, and I liked this place much better. I had thus *released* an old energy through the ascension process.

And yet, I will share with you another scenario creating a very different reaction within me than that of the one above. Over the years, I have become very frustrated with individuals who are not there for others, or who do not seem to care. Continually, they seem to care only for themselves, are very self-absorbed, have no time for anything but their own personal interests, and are rarely there for or concerned about others.

Over and over again, I would become mortified at this behavior. After all (smile), I was the one who cared about everyone in my family, listened and understood, always knew what was going on with everyone, stayed in continual contact, and was usually there when help was needed. I always felt like the only one unifying my family and friends.

So then, this seemingly opposing behavior from others went totally against everything I felt to be good, valued, and of the highest order! And it created continual frustration, anger, and feelings of mortification as well. How could others be so heartless, self-absorbed, and un-caring?!

I had an intense reaction, no doubt. Unity is very important to me, coming from a family where there was much abandonment present and living in a world where most don't "see," connect with, and acknowledge the faces and essences of their brothers and sisters. But what was occurring here was that I was imbalanced with my own energy. I needed to be more like others who seemed to be so very self-absorbed. Although they were out of balance as much as myself, my reaction was proof that I was still experiencing issues relating to abandonment, and not then, reacting with sadness or understanding that unity was still not present upon this planet. I had yet to *balance* an energy within me, and one that I would be keeping.

As energy cannot move higher until it fully integrates where it is now, we cannot step over certain phases of our evolutionary process. When we are complete with one phase, we are then able to move on to the next. In the more distant past, we created the same phases or steps, over and over as a planet. We did not seem to be able to get past many of them as a whole. Even though many of us incarnated individually and had wonderful experiences utilizing form, we were not able to affect the whole to a large or lasting degree, nor did we particularly want to. We were just here to experience energy in form. During these times, there was a predominance of darker and denser interfering energies...the energies that we ourselves embodied at one time or another during our experiences with utilizing form.

What is now different is that our plan for ascension is succeeding beautifully, and we are now moving forward as a whole. This is because *we all came at the same time* to ensure our success. ..*and,* we had a brilliant and all encompassing plan...*and,* we are now ready to wrap it all up, not to just be here experiencing form as we had done in many previous incarnations. We honestly did not know if this plan would work or not! Thus, many of us have the same agenda, are all in this together, and are really working as a team. In addition, the planet is moving into a new energetic space in the cosmos that is vibrating higher. Our spiritual evolutionary process is coming from without as well as within, as this is how all creation works. *Everyone* and *everything* is in on this plan, even though it may not seem like it at times! (Remember, darkness spurs on the willingness for change, so then, we are always all one and going in the same direction of love, even though we each have different roles. In other words, those embodying darkness are in on the plan, as their role is to spur the change. They are old souls as well, even though it may appear otherwise.)

As more and more of the masses begin to vibrate higher as a whole, more natural disasters will occur, more personal shake-ups will occur, and overall things will get much more intense for many....but mostly for those who are at lower vibrating rungs of the ascension ladder. This is because alignments are then needed....and everything on the planet earth will need to align with new and higher ways of being and living. Those who have gone ahead (i.e. having already experienced many shake-ups and re-alignments in years prior) and paved the way for others to follow, will instead experience more abundance, miracles, and the life of their wildest dreams (or their versions of Heaven on Earth).

Those on higher rungs of the evolutionary ladder will indeed experience internal adjustments as well, but not with the magnitude of those who are following as a whole. This is because those who are following have either not yet made choices that their souls have been guiding them to make, or because they have chosen to represent a part of the whole which agreed to hold the lower vibrating spaces while the way-showers moved ahead; thus creating a more gentle and step-by-step process. These adjustments for the way-showers primarily involve changes in the way each individual runs his/her energy, as more and more of our personality selves, or ego selves, is now dissipating and departing for some other reality far, far way. Generally speaking, this mostly involves a process of evolving into higher states of love, without so many life shake-ups.

Natural disasters, or cleansings, will occur in areas of land mass and within individuals as well. After a cleansing has occurred, such as a hurricane, flood, fire, or the like, then the specific area is then very ready to carry a much higher vibration. These cleansed areas will attract higher vibrating individuals and newly higher vibrating communities will begin to form. And sometimes, several cleansings are required as certain areas are not yet matching the vibration intended, or perhaps these areas of prior cleansings have been rebuilt utilizing the ways of the old reality.

When individuals experience a cleanse or "natural disaster" within, they also now vibrate higher as well, especially if they willingly agree to let go of old patterns and ways of making things happen. Many times I have witnessed individuals who experience a cleanse or release, but are not willing to go along with it. In this way, they are going against their soul plans....and this is a matter of choice. This is also when mismatching begins to occur between individuals and souls must then part ways.

So then, the ascension process is comprised of continual stepping stones, as we cannot go anywhere or evolve until we know, accept, and embody where we are now. We can only begin, then, with where we are now. And many times we like where we are, are not ready for yet *another* change, and can grow very weary from all the expansion, growth, movement, and losses! The ascension process keeps us on our toes indeed. But as we progress on our own personal journeys, things begin to get better and better. If we were to look back at who we were in times past, we would most likely see a very different person and wonder who that person was as we now do not remotely resemble them!

Yes, we are going somewhere most certainly, even though being in the moment and in the now is seemingly how to get there. Expansion is never ending...it is one of the laws of the universe. So then, because of the ascension process, we are seemingly always headed somewhere...and getting there by being where we are.

-•-

A shorter version:

We evolve in slow, gradual steps. Trying to push this process only serves to place us out of the natural alignment that the ascension process is designed to provide. After we are through releasing or balancing any lower vibrating energies within us, we are then very ready to move forward onto a new rung of the ascension ladder. The more we evolve as a planet, the higher we vibrate, and thus, we begin interacting more as a whole. When interacting more as a whole, we then begin expansion experiences more as a whole, and thus, things can seem to be getting worse or slowing down as we are more connected than ever before.

The shortest version:

The ascension process is designed to occur in small, gradual steps, involving us as individuals first and then progressing to more of the whole.

~ Where We Are Headed ~

Where are we headed, then, and what does the New Reality look like?

We are seemingly all going "there," whether we consciously want to or not. At our higher soul levels, we are very willing to be moving ahead, as we would not be on this planet now if we did not want to participate in the ascension process.

One of the most uncomfortable aspects of the ascension process relates to the fact that we evolve and expand within, while the outside reality has not yet caught up. Even though higher vibrating energies may be bombarding the planet and surround us at times, what surrounds us in form was created at a completely different vibrational time, or level of a now defunct reality to the one we are now vibrating within. We eventually create on the outside what we are vibrating on the inside, so the outside comes second. In addition, the collective outside is created by the masses, who must reach a certain critical mass as well as having a willingness to create change before a new world in the physical can eventually manifest. This takes time...and thus can cause great discomfort while we are seemingly out of alignment with where we are residing.

Yes, the contrast we feel can be fairly uncomfortable at best, and frequently results in various states of depression, anxiety, and feelings of no sense of place. We may feel lost, alone, with nowhere to go, and may not be able to get comfortable no matter how hard we try. These experiences of discomfort also stem from the fact that we agreed to go first. It is simply an aspect of being a way-shower and of embodying the new energies within ourselves for everything else to follow.

This phenomenon can also create states of isolation for many of us, as it is just too dar n uncomfortable out there. So at times, our only salvation seems to be to create our own personal sanctuaries within our homes, within our living spaces, and perhaps with a close circle of friends. It can even be difficult to find that close circle of friends as so may of us are evolving at different rates (and may have different soul plans as well)!

Although we are indeed headed toward a similar vision that many of us share, we must first embody it before it can fully manifest; and it can only fully manifest when the time is right, when all the phases are complete, and when we have touched upon each of the stepping stones, one by one.

My particular vision of a higher reality can be found in the book *Staying In Alignment* (which can be found at http://www.whatsuponplanetearth.com). This version of a higher reality can be met when a substantial amount of releasing and purging has been done, and when so much has been cleared away that what remains is the purer gold nugget of our true authentic selves, with a strong connection to Source, as well as a strong residence in a near total space of on-going creativity. This is what remains after so much of the lower and denser energies have vacated...a creative individual who is strongly and surely aware of his/her purpose, gifts, talents, and connection to Source and the whole.

A Higher Reality Book Excerpt From *Staying In Alignment*:

"So imagine this, if you will. You wake up in the morning, eager to begin creating, as creating, along with experiencing what you and others have created, is the reason and purpose for your residency on the planet Earth. In this way, you are supporting the purpose of the Earth, as she exists as a playground for creation and experience. Creating and experiencing then places you in alignment with the earth.

You feel the sun streaming through the openings in your home, touching you and dancing upon your face, as you awaken to a new day. The sun loves to bring harmony and warmth, align with the plants and earth organisms, and support all life as it sustains it. Your home is warm when you awake, as the day before, the sun had left the beauty of its' heat within your passive solar heated thermal mass walls. Eating foods sustained by the sun and utilizing the warmth of the sun, then places you in alignment with her purpose.

Your home is made of the purest forms of the elements of the earth. The types of soil and elements from nature that are nearest to your home are what sustains and creates your home. There is much beauty within your home as well, as magnificent creations made from the earth embody and embellish your sacred space. Amazing, unique works of art fill this space, and you feel great whenever you are in it.

Sacred geometry can be found dispersed throughout your home and community as well, as it immediately aligns you through the simplicity of symbolism. In this way, you are living in alignment with the earth.

As you walk through your home, you go through handmade doors and into your passive solar greenhouse. You had opened these doors late the day before, in order to allow the natural heat embodied there to gravitate into your home and sustain its' warmth as night progressed. As you look around your greenhouse, you select just the right organic food to prepare for your breakfast. The food you select is delighted to be supporting you through its' nourishment, as this is its' intended purpose. And in alignment with the sun, the earth, and the rain that sustained it through your harmonious rain harvesting system, is now ready for you. It knows that as it serves to sustain your body, it will again return in another form, to enjoy the process of the cycle of life. All is in order, as this food joyously prepares itself for the next phase of its' journey.

The day progresses as you occupy yourself with your joys and passions. You are busy creating most all of the time. You create what you are about and what lights you up. In this way, you are in perfect alignment with self. You absolutely know who you are, what you are here to contribute, and how you will contribute this special and unique essence of yourself. There is never a confusing moment of straying from your true purpose, as aligning with it has become effortless. You know that you are in alignment with self because what you create makes you feel absolutely wonderful, you lose track of time while creating, it is effortless for you, you are very good at it, and there is a never-ending expanse of possibilities that arise from being in this pocket of creativity.

After awhile of creating, you decide to stroll through your village. On your brief journey, you encounter another, who offers you precisely what you currently need, through the higher order of like energies attracting like energies. And you seem to have something to offer this individual as well. You are both so very grateful for this meeting and hug each other in gratitude as you lovingly share a special and unique connection. An additional connection through your eyes takes you to even higher realms of memory. This is because you are one, and as your eyes engage each other, you remember this and your love for one another then increases even more.

Before you left your sacred space of home, where the alignments were even more specific to who you are, you had just completed a creative project that you will be contributing to your community. This creative project holds the energy of what your community is all about, therefore supporting it in all ways, as you support yourself...all in perfect alignment. The residents of your village have been eagerly awaiting this creation that arrived through your expertise and passion, and know without exception that it will serve to enhance all of the whole. You are very highly revered for your talents and contribution, and each and every individual in your community knows exactly who you are and what you are about. They are all so very grateful for your existence...and you for theirs as you greatly appreciate and need their contributions as well. You are very aware that you could not survive without them.

Being at the threshold of a new creative adventure now, you find yourself gravitating to the center of your village, where a sacred space has been created by all the residents who reside in your community. This space embodies a higher energy, as it is comprised of the combination and culmination of the energies of each of the residents of your community.

While you bask in this space, you suddenly become inspired to create something new and exciting. This new creation is so you, in all ways, and yet is something that has never been created before. With the conception of a new idea firmly in place, you then decide to bask for awhile and just *be*. Lying on a riverbank, you are joined by a deer, a hawk, a lizard, some happily growing wildflowers, beautiful clouds in the sky, and eventually some community members join you as well. As you all lie in a meadow together, your heads resting upon each other's bellies as you gaze at the white billowing clouds above, you are in total contentment with all that is. Eventually, off you go to share a meal together... a meal that has been created through the loving and purposeful energies of another who is in their joy and passion through cooking. You are all so grateful for this scrumptious meal, as you express your caring and love to its' creator. In this way, you have been in alignment with your new idea for creating, with nature, with others, and with a delicious meal!

After eating, all of you decide to gather at a community meeting space, which is under the stars and resting upon an energy spot of great expression and expansion. The architecture of this space is magnificent, as it was created by some of your brothers and sisters, and is comprised of elements of the earth, all creating a beautiful space of artistic expression. A performance is beginning, and it involves some of the many gifts and talents of the residents of your village. Beautiful music is experienced, as well as dance, art, and many other extraordinary talents that keep you all in a space of joy and gratitude for the gifts that only others can bring. You are deeply amazed at this extraordinary talent, as it brings you to tears while you gregariously applaud after each expression is presented. "How do they do that?" you wonder in awe.

As you return home to your own specialized sacred space, an owl guides your way and keeps you company, along with any special friends who may reside with you. While out in the night air, you experience a shooting star that has a grand and exciting message for you. When you finally come into your home, you feel as though you are still communing with the cosmos, as there are many skylights in your home, and even an observatory on the top floor. This particular evening, a magnificent planetary alignment can be seen through the portals of your home, and in this way you feel very in tune and lined up with the support and energies that these celestial bodies are offering you. They are so blissfully happy to be a part of your reality, and gladly and joyously shine their brilliance into your home. They are a part of your life, as you are a part of theirs.

While laying your head to rest upon a pillow of feathers that were lovingly contributed by your winged friends, you realize that someone is there in your bedroom. As you open to their presence, you are greeted by a being from the stars who has a request. A group of star beings would like to commune for a short while with your community, as they need your special energy and they have things to offer your community as well. They would like to join you with news from afar which they know you would love to hear. As a representative of your community who serves to communicate and commune with the star beings, you easily agree to this request and prepare to notify the community of this impending celebration and gathering. The communion is solidified, and you then blissfully fall asleep in what feels like the wings of angels, as they gently rock you to and fro. And you may be cuddling next to your favorite soul companion as well!"

What new ways are we now being encouraged to embody within us, that will place us in alignment with this scenario?

And what do the steps on our journey to this New Reality look like?

- -

A shorter version:

We are headed toward a reality where we ultimately connect to much higher vibrating things. As much of the old and denser energies are purged, released, and balanced, we are then left with a whole consisting of wonderful and beautiful things. Each and every need will be met my another's passion and purpose, while we contribute our passion and purpose as well. The remainder of the time we will spend enjoying ourselves in the company of our brothers and sisters.

The shortest version:

The earth will ultimately consist of a perfect interaction of higher vibrating energies.

~Keys To Living In The New
Energies ~

Much was illuminated that special day out in the wilderness, when I was so blessed to be surrounded by the higher realms in totality while in the physical.

It is not specifically through dimensional hopping or through psychic visions that these keys and new, higher ways of being are revealed to us. As we progress through the ascension process, we gradually begin to embody many aha's and epiphanies. We begin to see things differently, as our veils of density begin to slowly disappear. I love the definition of epiphany: "A comprehension or perception of reality by means of a sudden intuitive realization." *A comprehension or perception of reality.* How very perfect. So many times, we can suddenly find that what we thought was a higher way of being, was actually not. We may think that we have been doing the right or best thing with all our knowingness, but when we begin to vibrate higher, we may be mortified when we discover that we have been way off the mark. All this time we never knew. This is why I continually say that the higher realms is not what we thought it was....and we do not know until we get there!

So, as we slowly but surely release and purge the lower and more densely vibrating energies within us (or our many mis-perceptions), we then become much more connected to Source. This also grants us a new residency in a higher vibrating reality, allowing us through new gates, as we are now a match for the higher vibrating energies on the other side.

We are continually in transition, so in this way, some of us are in one space and many of us are in another.

What are the keys to staying in alignment and to living in harmony in a more higher vibrating reality? And what are the new ways of living and being on this new and "other side" that we now have such easy and effortless access to?

Although there are many stages and levels of dimensional hierarchies now available to us, and although many of us are at differing levels as we are always right where we need to be, the new ways of living and being offered here are applicable at most every level.

Getting Through The Gate

Accessing the new reality greatly involves focusing on *it*, instead of what remains of our old and lower vibrating manifestations of the 3D reality. And it greatly involves our perceptions of what we believe reality to be. In the higher realms, even more so than in the old 3D world, it is all about perceptions. We create what we perceive to be true. And what we have perceived up until recently has been through the filter of a lower vibrating human. We need not do this anymore. But know as well, that if all of our mis-perceptions disappeared in one fell swoop, we would be traumatized and most likely go into shock. We could feel violated, our trust, foundation, and security would be threatened, and we might feel as though we had nothing much to hold onto. This is why the ascension process is so gradual, even though it may not feel that way at times!

You will find some common mis-perceptions of the old 3D reality woven through-out the pages of this book, and thus, may then find yourself as well in any given stage.

The biggest and most pronounced thing that I have noticed about the higher realms, is that a higher realms reality is now right on top of us. We have simply just not been focused there. This pocket of energy, or different dimension, is available to us through sheer focus alone. Most of the time, we are busy focusing on what we think we need to do to *get* there, or on what we think we must accomplish now in our lives in order to survive, or we may even find ourselves continuing to focus on what is wrong with others, instead of focusing on their gifts and talents. This is because we have bought into one *big illusion* that was created in the 3D world.

This is the illusion that says that everything is outside of us. This is the illusion that says we create everything by using money. This is the illusion that encourages us to focus on manifesting, instead of on *being*. This is the illusion that says that we are all separate and responsible for ourselves only. This is the illusion that says that we should be somewhere else other than where we are, as we are not yet "there," wherever we think "there" is, and on and on. We seem to be focusing on everything *except* the higher realms, where we are actually now residing! We are lost in a merry-go-round of lower vibrating thought and limitation.

I will never forget the clarity that was present when I could see it all. A higher vibrating reality was right here, right now, just sitting there, waiting to be noticed. It was as if no one was paying any attention to this beautiful "thing" that was right in front of us....just begging to be utilized and visited! Yes, we are here....right now.

So then, *focusing* on being in the higher realms, seeing and acknowledging it, knowing we are now residing there, and accepting and utilizing a new way of living and being, is the first step and primary tool in accessing this higher vibrating reality.

Focusing on the higher realms ways of being and living, and knowing they are different from the prior 3D reality, while truly believing and trusting these higher ways to be true and to exist now, will grant us immediate access.

Yes, the higher realms are just waiting for us to notice them, and wondering where the heck we are!

The Keys

There are several basic keys to living (or rather *being*) in our current levels of higher realms reality, and several stepping stones to meet, which will help us to best utilize these new and awesome energies for maximum benefit and enjoyment. After we accept that we are really and truly here now, and thus begin to spend more time focusing on and accepting this new reality, we can then move more fully into it.

Remember......"Oh, hi! I stepped right on you, and didn't notice you were there! You were so quiet and subtle, and I have only been noticing what seems to scream at me as a thorn in my side, or what is seemingly *wrong*! How long have you been there in all your beauty, and why have I never noticed you until now?"

As we progress ever more fully into higher vibrating and more evolved human beings, we come to know that there is no longer a feminine or masculine, divine or otherwise. The more we balance and let go of the denser energies within us, the more we become one, whole, or rather a more androgynous being. In times past, the masculine embodied the male form and the feminine the female form. A following phase created males who embodied more feminine energies and females who embodied more masculine energies. And soon, we will all just be wonderful and delightful companions, with no need to differentiate what is masculine or feminine, and the labels will be dropped altogether. This awareness and occurrence is happening now.

For our purposes here, I will be utilizing older and more densely vibrating labels of masculine and feminine, in order to differentiate the differences in action and being. These keys and steeping stones will be described in detail in the following section.

Keys of Being: The Feminine

- Shifting into a new way of being and thinking / navigating the dimensions.
- We always have everything we need.
- Accessing the higher realms through the earth.
- Not taking things personally.
- Creativity in the higher realms.
- Focus and clarity.
- Living effortlessly with no struggle or suffering.

- Shutting the door behind us.

Stepping Stones On Our Path: The Masculine

- Knowing who we are.
- Defining our path.
- Connecting with our soul teams and new communities.
- Identifying our geographical home on earth.
- Living without the need for money.
- Setting up our store fronts.
- Connecting with the Star Beings.
- Knowing our path of service.
- Finding our Heaven.

~ Keys of Being: the Feminine ~

The energies of the New Reality require a different state of *being.* In order for higher vibrating energies of a new reality to be utilized and implemented to their greatest advantage, it can greatly help if we are in alignment with them, and if we understand how they work.

As mentioned earlier in this book, focusing our attention on the New Reality is a key component of being there. If we do not yet realize that we have arrived in a higher vibrating reality, we will continue to create and accept the ways of being that existed in a lower vibrating reality. ..and they won't feel very good! In addition, the higher the dimension or vibration of the reality we are in, the more intensified the energies become.

This is why we begin to manifest so much more of what we think about, how we vibrate (or who we are and how we perceive things), and so forth, the more we evolve and expand (or the higher the dimension we find ourselves in). In this way, most of us would thus want more of a good thing, instead of more of an unpleasant thing.

Everything is magnified in the higher realms indeed, so we will really know who we are and how we run our energy by what begins showing up for us in profound and exaggerated ways the more we bump up into the higher realms. This also offers us a wonderful opportunity to make changes within if need be; and "need be" will eventually become mandatory the more we neglect, ignore, or are unwilling to adjust ourselves and our patterns. Ouch! This is also why our ascension process seems to take so long.....if much of everything was magnified before we purged and released a fair amount, we would be experiencing hell on Earth instead of Heaven.

Shifting Into A New Way Of Being And Thinking

Navigating the dimensions, or moving to any different reality for that matter, simply requires a shift in focus, attention, and thought. It is in this way that we are able to drive our vehicles and steer them to the destination of our desires. A change in thought and focus then, is all that is required.

When I look through the dimensions, I usually focus my intention on being there, and a new pocket of energy will immediately open up for my arrival. This is all that is required, along with leaving our old spaces as well. With less and less density now present, this way of "traveling" is easier than ever before. Different realities exist everywhere and many times they are neighbors that live right next door to us. We need only notice who lives next door, knock on their doors, and if we are respectful and allowing, we will usually be easily admitted with open arms. Or we can choose to ignore what is next door, and it will not be granted access into our reality.

At one point during my years of writing the energy alerts, I began to receive an abundance of unpleasant and angry emails from readers. Some of them were what I felt to be highly disrespectful and downright rude. I seriously considered resigning, as I felt I was being beat up and certainly unappreciated, and was not too sure that I wanted this group in my arena at all. Although I understood that it was all about them and not particularly about me, it was wearing me out none-the-less. During that time as well, I was having concerns about offering my books in e-book format. With the strong network of spiritual seekers, I felt that e-books would be passed around for free (I did not resonate with all the controls offered on some e-books), and this would be unfair to me as well as to my publisher. In addition, there was an "out of control" aspect to the e-book situation as well. I give a lot of my writings away without requiring a payment, and my books are the only aspect of my work where I require a payment.

With advice and suggestions from a friend providing a different perspective, this situation soon resolved itself. I was not very comfortable with this unpleasant group of readers being attracted to my work, and I also did not want readers offering the e-books to many others free of charge who really did not value what they were reading. I felt lost in a sea of no integrity! My new perspective was this: I decided to focus on and welcome readers who had integrity, who were respectful, and who appreciated what I had to offer...and there were still many of those out there (but they are usually the quiet ones). In this way, no one else existed for me. So then, if readers were exhibiting dis-respectful behavior, I simply would not consider them my readers. And knowing that all my financial needs had been continually met for several years, also allowed me to realize that I would be fine, even if this activity occurred. It was not about the money. I simply would not allow these readers into my consciousness.

I continued to write, to offer what I had to offer while in my joy and bliss, and thus, the readers who then entered my space began to change. Oh, the power of ignoring what we do not choose to focus on! It turned everything around for me...this new perspective. I was then able to value, appreciate, allow, tune into, and welcome only the readers which I chose to see, instead of any others who were still out there oblivious to me. They might still be there, but they now seemed to exist in a completely different reality from my own. When the energies are more challenging than usual, I still receive the angry and disrespectful emails, and they still wear me out at times, but all in all, this process seems to work wonders for allowing me to continue on with my contribution to the planet.

In the higher realms, we need not create with intentional controls. Our needs can be met without knowing or controlling how. And this involves continuing to do what we love, while ignoring the peripheral energies that may at times surround us.

One ascension symptom which continues on as we progress is the one which says, "What was I just doing? I know I came into this room for something!" Or perhaps while you are driving down the road, you simply cannot remember where you are going. Or even the most common one of completely forgetting your thought before you finish a sentence, and especially the names of most of anything. This particular ascension symptom stems from the fact that the higher we vibrate, the less we hold onto. In the higher realms, energy moves in and out very quickly. What we no longer hold in our consciousness will simply cease to exist. In this way, we can create fresh and new at any given moment by simply directing our focus. This is how we navigate in the higher realms and how we can access them as well. Just like the situation with my readers, not allowing them into my reality or consciousness greatly helped in creating a much more comfortable experience.

Not holding onto things in our consciousness is one way of being in the New Reality, and focusing on things or *keeping* them in our consciousness is yet another.

Early in 2007, as mentioned earlier in this book, I was blessed to connect with a man who had a fair amount of knowledge about the ancient ruins in the area where I lived. Having lived here in the American Southwest for many years, he knew about hidden areas of ancient springs and ancient pueblos, shrines, and the like. These areas were not widely known to many, and some to no one. He also knew a lot about artifacts, the ancient cultures, and how they were connected. Soon after we connected, I had the pleasure of embarking with him on regular adventures to these ancient sites. While hanging around with him, he taught me what to look for, how to see many things that were hidden to most, and much else.

After our first adventure, I was walking along the river in an ancient area where I had walked at least three or four times per week for the last year. I stopped at one point to simply breathe in the air on this cold day, and just be. As I stood there on a spot that I had traversed so many times, I found myself gazing across the river at a rocky cliff. Lo and behold, there right in front of me, was an ancient wall. This wall had been there all along, and I had never even seen it! When we are trained where to place our intent, or even in regard to what we continually embody within us, we will begin to see so many different realities that have been at our disposal all along, only we may have never noticed them before. This is the way it is in regard to our focus and intent to be in the higher realms. The higher realms have been there all along, but we have not been focusing our intent in regard to seeing them. The same is true for solutions to any dilemmas. They are always there all along, but we may get caught up in our limited thinking and not see the unlimited possibilities of what is right in front of us.

Locking into the New Reality which is right in front of us is a key component then, of our new state of being. Along with being a now higher vibrating human, focusing on where we want to be is necessary to get us through the gates. And as we begin to vibrate higher and higher and progress in our process, we will not need to have much of an intent or a focus, as we will simply *be* where we are vibrating, very naturally. Intent naturally becomes an unneeded and very unnecessary step in the higher realms. The state of just *being* creates very naturally on its own, and intent becomes much too contrived and planned...much too lengthy a process for the quick manifesting we can find ourselves involved with now.

The old 3D death process involved a very sudden release of any lower vibrating energies within us. This sudden release thus created a new residency in the higher realms. Through the ascension or spiritual evolutionary process we are currently undergoing, we are experiencing the same, only very gradually and while still in human form. In addition, when an individual crossed over through the old 3D death process, there was always the opportunity for each individual to create whatever he or she chose. In this way, some became stuck in a revolving door of continually creating in relation to their mis-perceptions and beliefs. This usually happens with an individual who is strong willed and narrowly focused. These souls may have thought that they were indeed stuck or perhaps in hell instead of Heaven.

So then, this is still a possibility for those who have arrived in a higher dimension while still in form. We can choose to create miracles, peace, joy, love, and have an effortless ease with all things, or we can continue to create a reality of a lower vibrating nature, even though we are now in the next dimension.

Shifting into a new way of being and thinking, and keeping our focus there, is one of the first steps of being in a higher dimension, until we are able to be there naturally with no intent or focus necessary.

Whenever I spend more time than I normally do with things relating to the "old" reality, I can feel a real difference. It is as if I have regressed, or perhaps bought into those old ideas from the 3D existence. I usually begin to feel disconnected from all the beauty, peace, and feelings of ease, relaxation, and connection to a different world. I can only take so much of this other lower dimensional reality, and then I have to call it a day. And being that we have not yet shifted *completely* over into higher ways of living in every way possible, there are times when most of us must still participate in the old ways from time to time.

We can stay in alignment with the higher realms in regard to shifting into a new way of being and thinking, by making it a priority in our lives. For me, if I forget that I am now residing in the higher realms, I will feel out of balance, or as if I am on a short trip and cannot wait to get back. I feel like a sunken ship, lost in the depths and density of a deep dis-connected reality. This is my barometer, and a high sign that I need to return. If I begin to feel pressure, stress, or that I am too much at the helm, I don't feel so good either, and am then very inspired to get back to the better feeling ways of effortlessness, great amounts of time in creativity, simplicity, and a wonderful flow with no timelines, hoops to jump through, or confining boxes.

One way to stay in alignment with new ways of being and thinking is to simply pull back and remove ourselves from what we "appear" to be experiencing. In other words, realizing that the old ways are just an illusionary game, not allowing them to consume us and not buying into them, can help as well. If we can accept that these old ways are still here for a short time, while we are evolving, without resisting them, and if we can know that we only need visit them for short periods of time, we can more easily stay in alignment with a higher way.

For me, I live the far majority of the time in my own world, connecting to nature, creativity, and spend very little time with involvements of the other world. If you are one who cannot do this due to a job, for instance, try and focus on anything in your arena there that vibrates high....the best qualities of co-workers, helping others, the scenery, or anything that makes you feel good. By being yourself and shining your light, you will naturally bring up the vibration around you.....very *un-intentionally*. Finding something to connect to that vibrates higher will also allow you to feel a part of the whole, and not so much of an alien.

Looking and focusing above what the illusion is presenting, will also serve to clarify what is indeed actually occurring. A few years ago, when I decided it was time to purchase some land, I had a wonderful experience of focusing and being in a higher level of the older 3D reality. I had found some land with a doublewide trailer on it, a well in place, a wind turbine, a solar panel, and fencing on twelve acres. I was initially attracted to this land because so much of what I would need to do was already in place. There was even a doublewide to provide temporary housing while I was building my natural home. I had picked up some rather uncomfortable energy there that had to do with some Native American burial grounds and forbidden energy...an unwelcome sort of energy, but my bull headed Taurus nature supported me in forging ahead anyway. In this way then, all was not ideal and I should have known better. At that time I was one *weary* lightworker, and ready to simply relax and receive, so having so much already in place in regard to this property was quite appealing.

Eventually, I was not comfortable with the energy there. My non-physical star companion had said that this land was forbidden, and that another individual I knew would find me another piece of land. For several reasons, this made absolutely no sense at the time, so I finally just said to the Universe, "If this land is not in my best interest, please block me from connecting to it." Within 15 minutes, my real estate broker called and said that the seller had decided not to sell after all. If I had not known that I was indeed being protected, I probably would have been disappointed or thought that something was wrong. And within a day, this other individual did find me some land, and this land was a much better fit. I'm sure that many of you have had similar experiences in this regard. No new news here.

By not focusing and buying into what is seemingly right in front of us, and instead focusing on a higher reality of our experiences, we can then be more in alignment with higher ways of being and thinking. When we can truly believe that things are always being divinely orchestrated at our soul levels, it is then that we can open to magic, miracles, and more of an effortless existence.

During the ascension process, we are *always* taken care of. Things are being navigated by our souls and our loving non-physical companions. So in this regard, things may not always be what they appear to be. At higher levels, all is always in divine and perfect order.

The more we progress up the ascension ladder, the more we evolve past this stage of asking the universe to show us this or that. We thus begin to have an ability to see things immediately...to see through the din and density of the lower vibrations, and to actually *become* the universe ourselves... rather than surrendering to it and placing the power outside of ourselves. We are then *becoming* more and more of our souls and very conscious of it. This is just another wonderful and exciting thing about our spiritual evolutionary process...it just seems to get better and better the more we evolve.

 ## Staying in Alignment With New Ways of Being and Thinking

- We can choose to focus on a higher reality (or explanation) of what our experiences may be showing us.

- We can allow only what we choose to allow to remain in our consciousness.
- We can spend as little time as possible in the illusory world of old 3D manifestations.
- We can create a life in another world of our choosing. (Eventually, we are able to live and support ourselves through our passions, as we spend the majority of our time in our personal sanctuaries. We will eventually expand from there into small local areas of residence, or our new communities.)

After we gain access to the higher dimensions through our focus and through our new higher vibrating selves, what are some of these new ways of being that thrive in the higher dimensions?

We Always Have Everything We Need

Knowing and realizing that we always have everything we need, is perhaps one of the most key elements of higher dimensional living and being. We are never missing anything, or incomplete, or even experiencing lack, even though many times we think that we are.

"If only I had this or that, my life would be completely different." How many times have we had a thought such as this? And is it true?

I first began seeing and experiencing this concept several years ago during the unusual planetary alignment of May 5, 2000. A higher energy had bombarded the planet during this time, and this message became quite clear, as the months of May, June, and August of 2000 were a time of higher vibrating reality for a while, if one chose to go there. (At different times on the planet, an opening or portal to a higher dimension is created, although it does not stay open permanently at that time. We are then given an opportunity to connect to, or to anchor into this energy and thus utilize it or "remember" it until it becomes a normal state of being for us.)

During that time, I had removed myself from the outer world, and was basking in my inner world. For about three months, I spent time in creativity and nature, with no connection to the outside world (I was not working, had no source of income, but received all I needed, even though seemingly quite accidentally!). Slowly I began to get this message, as every time I thought that I needed something from the store for a creative project, I would find that I already had it. It was right there in my home, but I was looking at acquiring it on the outside. This happened over and over again. Either I accidentally found the item I needed somewhere in my house (and it had been there all along, and for a long while as well!), or it would miraculously appear as a gift from another. Eventually, I began to get the idea, and to really get the message. Something was going on here, and it had become quite evident.

The next time this pattern became evident was in 2006, when our vibration as a whole had reached a higher level, and this way of being was then ready to become a permanent reality for me. I lived then in a very small community with few stores. Each time that I thought I needed something specific, and assumed that I would never find it there, I would either drive three hours to the closest bigger community, or even wait until I was visiting relatives in southern California, where there is every kind of store imaginable.

Over and over, the same thing would happen. I always found exactly what I needed *right there* in my little town, and could never seem to find it in the bigger towns and cities that had all the seeming opportunities! It began to get humorous, as I would find these things that one would never expect....and they would be right in my own back yard. I eventually came to realize that I need not ever leave my area of matching vibration, as it was supporting me in very way.

The next message in this arena came a few months later. One day while I was out in a vast area of wilderness with my non-physical companion, I had missed conversing with him of late, so I asked him, "Is there anything that I need to know at this time?" His immediate reply was, "You are not utilizing the resources around you." Well, this really opened up my eyes even further to this concept. And the message was again the same. We always have everything that we need, but we are accustomed to thinking we are experiencing lack, and therefore do not see what is right in front of us.

In this case, I was wishing I had some help finding land from a knowledgeable person, as well as knowing it was time to reach more individuals regarding my work. I knew these things were my next steps, and I was not willing to wear all of the hats. Suddenly, it became very clear to me that my friend, who was also the owner of the ranch where I boarded my alpacas, was also a real estate broker. In addition, the husband of the husband/wife team who are my publishers, had been an internet marketing consultant for years, and had offered his services to me early on. In both cases, the gifts of these individuals were free of charge, and they had both been in my space for several months. I had overlooked them, as I was focused on my lack there-of, and used to doing everything myself! And I never believed in the concept of marketing anyway, but he had written to me early on offering his help if I had wanted to find ways of assisting others who may have not connected with me yet. (In the end, I never needed any marketing changes, but it was great to talk to this kind and wonderful man anyway.)

As we evolve higher and higher, this concept will become more and more refined. We will soon find that we need not ever leave our geographical area of personal sanctuary or our land, as both will provide absolutely everything we need. And in times to come, we will find that "local" will be a word we utilize and live with as a very integral part of our lives. The impending natural disasters and upheavals from the old ways that are crashing very rapidly now, will serve to support and truly create this concept, as the old governmental structures will no longer be able to assist. All will be in divine and perfect order. Local vibrates with local. We attract what we are vibrating, so local will be very much in harmony with where we find ourselves residing. We will each be right where we need to be, in matching vibration, and be totally sustained with everything local. This is the higher way of being that will be created through the fall.

The above scenarios exist at certain levels of reality, but as we progress in our spiritual evolutionary process, we will eventually find that we have simply given up the state of being called "wanting," and we may not even remember when this occurred.

Believing that we do not have all that we need requires a belief in separation. In the 3D energies and vibrations, things were much denser. This density created a great separation with most of everything. We were just not able to see through this density, and to see what was right in front of us. As we begin vibrating higher, we can then begin to see what we have never been able to see before. The boundaries begin to disappear, the walls to come down, and unity seemingly begins to magically appear (as well as a feeling of vulnerability without our usual walls!).

One way to stay in alignment with the concept of having everything we need, is to accept and know that all our needs are always met, and that there is a solution, answer, and seemingly missing piece already in existence, only we may have just not connected to it yet. What we need is absolutely there, no question about it, but we have just not allowed it into our space quite yet. As we begin to shift and expand, we are then able to connect to things like never before, through the most substantial and important way of being in the Universe.....like energies attracting like energies. When we begin to vibrate higher, and to lose many of our mis-perceptions and bull headed beliefs that we were so stuck on and attached to (or ego selves), we are then able to attract and connect to incredible and perfect things much more easily. With much of these lower vibrating energies now gone, the road is then clear. And this way of being really relates to beloved soul companions and our brothers and sisters as well. The form or package which surrounds what it is that we really and truly need or want, does not remotely matter. It is what is inside that truly counts....the true gift is within the wrapping only sometimes we do not see it.

Getting out of the way, through knowing with certainly that the Universe will provide all we need, allows then, a space to open that can then be filled. When we strive to do everything ourselves, we block this flow of support. And thinking that what we need has to arrive in a very specific way, can hinder this connection as well. It is our denser self (or ego) that has to have things "just so." As we begin vibrating higher, we find that what we really and truly need are higher vibrating things, such as love, beauty (in any form), unity, and the like. The rest is inconsequential. The details begin to dissipate the higher we vibrate. Purity is what remains. So what is left after so much has been released, lost, and perhaps never manifested, are these pure vibrations of simplicity found in the higher realms. And this is when Heaven and bliss truly arrive for us. And this is what the ascension process strives to create... the loss of everything but higher vibrating Heaven and bliss.

Several years ago, when I was living in a small community in Arizona for about a year, I found that I needed a medical practitioner. I had not been to a doctor or healer for several years, but was taking a medication that needed to be monitored, and thus, I needed to see a doctor every year. I asked a friend if she knew of anyone, and she referred me to a team of two nurse practitioners that she liked. So I made an appointment.

First, I was told that they were not taking new patients, but my application would be reviewed and they would get back to me in about a week. The next day the office called and said that I was welcome to come on board as a new patient. When the nurse practitioner came into the examining room, she exclaimed, "I can't believe that Karen Bishop is sitting in my examining room." "Do you greet all your patients in this valuing way?" I asked.

Well, it turned out that she had read my book, was an energy healer, and very metaphysical. In this small town of 3,000 people, each and every one of my new acquaintances thus far was either a lightworker and did not know it, a rancher, one of Mormon faith, an environmentalist, an artist, or just a great person. No one was really familiar with my writing...they just knew that I was a writer and was not familiar at all with what I wrote about.

My new medical practitioner had been in an office that I had parked in front of many, many times, and I had not even known that she was there. We ended up meeting at her home a week or so later, and I was so glad to know that she was in the area. Not one to intentionally seek out a spiritual or metaphysical community, I had connected to her none-the-less. Both our purposes were very connected, as she was part of the team involved with setting up our golden city of light....even though it was not yet time. We had both been drawn to this area of great portals and magnificent light. And having an allopathic medical practitioner that knew all about ascension symptoms was truly divine. She was right in my space all along, only I had never noticed or needed her...

 ## Staying in Alignment with Knowing We Have Everything We Need

- We can get out of our own way, and not try to make everything happen ourselves. Source will do it for us if we give Source a chance.
- By knowing and trusting that we will always be taken care of...remember, we are the ones creating and experiencing the ascension process, thus, we were not meant to suffer. We may not consciously have all the answers, but Source does. We need only trust, allow, and follow the path that is being

revealed to us...the path where the doors seem to open.

- We can remember that we are loved beyond measure, and the universe *wants* to provide all our needs.

- We can remember that we need very little, as some of the time we feel a need to fill up a hole within us by acquiring things. What we really and truly need, or what is in alignment with our true selves, will arrive effortlessly in a wonderfully supportive way on a very regular basis.

- By knowing that much of the time, what we need is right in front of us, but we are not noticing it, as we are used to believing in lack and thus expecting just that.

- We can connect with local community, which will provide everything locally enabling us to "stay put" with no reaching, extending, or needing to make things happen...thus creating a state of *being*.

- By eventually realizing that what we need is very simple, and usually involves the love of others, companionship of loving friends, and simply *being*. Thus we finally realize that we are whole and complete right now and always have been.

This concept of always having everything we need extends to higher ways of living with the earth as well. In the following section, you will come to see how the earth herself and the celestial bodies were designed to offer us our every need, if only we choose to connect with them and utilize their bounty. And they have been here all along.

Accessing the Higher Realms Through the Earth

The earth is most certainly ascending, as is every living thing that exists upon and within her. Holding onto her then, or integrating with her as much as possible, can give us a free ride through the dimensions as well as giving us a more comfortable ride through the ascension process.

Our beautiful Earth contains portals as well; portals which offer openings to the higher dimensions. This earth is without a doubt the blue jewel of all time. It is here that we have chosen to experience our spiritual evolutionary journey back to Source. It is here that we have all come together as the original souls who first created this planet as a playground for experience and creation in form. Yes, the earth is the key.

The higher realms are not "up there," "out there," or somewhere else. Similar to the concept of having everything we need right now, we are able to access the higher realms then, directly through the earth herself. The higher realms, then, are *here*.

And in this way, we can come to know that we are right where we need to be. We are truly in Heaven...we need not go anywhere to get there. There is nothing missing. We are not waiting to "leave," go back home to our star families, and not even having an experience of suffering through some sort of belief in separation. We are not actually separated at all. Many key players from our star families from home are here with us right now. The remaining members are eagerly waiting and watching us progress through this amazing process. Those closest to us...those souls who were created at the same time we were, are *here*. We are then, not alone. All the love we have ever experienced in our entire existence is *here*. It is not necessarily then, back home.

In this way, we need not go anywhere, as everything we have longed for is right here in our spaces...including Source. The density of the lower vibrations has just prohibited us from seeing it. Yes, we are evolving back to Heaven, only Heaven is *here*. And as we begin to vibrate higher and higher, we will begin to connect more and more, and unity will become more prevalent than ever. This is happening right *now*...can you see it? As the ascension process continues to break down our walls of density, wear away much of our ego states, and allows us the simplicity of higher ways of being and "seeing," unity is very much a natural by-product.

So then, a key component and way of *being* in the higher realms, is knowing that we get there by being *here*. Just as Heaven is not really outside of us, as it is within us, Heaven in the physical form is right here on Earth as well. Heaven then, is not somewhere far away up in the sky that we go to when we die. Heaven is here, only it lies in a higher vibrating dimension without many of the mis-perceptions we have possessed for so long.

Because we may not know that we are now residing in a higher dimension, we may completely miss seeing it, even though it is right in front of us. The same is true for the earth as well. When we are able to fully connect to the earth, we are then able to connect to the higher realms. The earth, then, is a pivotal key. A society that spends time in busyness, involved with much relating to making money, running continuous errands, or other preoccupations that are not related at all to the earth, is not very connected. Having the earth go unnoticed in our everyday lives is a sad thing indeed. In the higher realms, what we are living within and upon is greatly integrated into our everyday lives and most certainly acknowledged and highly revered...it is a part of our whole.

The earth is also greatly connected to the celestial bodies, and we can also, then, utilize this connection too. The earth and the celestial bodies all work together as a team, and we are part of this team as well. The sun, the moon, the planets, and the earth provide everything we need to sustain ourselves. If we can learn to utilize their energies and the gifts that they offer us, we are then in total alignment with the higher realms.

The more we are in alignment with who we are and with what surrounds us, the more harmony we create and the more we are connected to Source. Alignments (or harmony) allow for Source energy to flow through us, as alignments create a vortex or opening that serves to connect to the higher vibrating energies of Source. So then, aligning with as much as we can which is in our space, and which vibrates the highest, can only serve to create a wonderful portal within us.

 ## Staying In Alignment With the Earth

- We can spend as much time as possible out in nature. The nature kingdom is aligned as well and knows exactly who it is and what it is doing. The parts of the nature kingdom that are no longer in alignment simply know how to leave. And while they are here, they know how to be what they are and what they were intended to be...in their purest and simplest version...just shining their light. This is a simple process of life and evolution. Energy infuses itself into form, stays as long as things are in alignment with it, and then simply leaves. Nature knows this cycle and accepts it. So in this way, nature is always in alignment with the higher vibrations. If you cannot spend time in nature as much as you would like, then bring nature to you by bringing it into your space...rocks, plants, animals, fountains, etc. What I love about nature, is that it has a clear, precise, and un-muddled vibration of knowing its purpose and identity, and is very simply who and what it is, un-swayed by the opinions of others! (This state of being is what we human beings are evolving into as well.)

- We can surround ourselves with as many pristine and earth centered creations as possible, whether in our homes, in our gardens, or elsewhere....going "natural" is the key. I use baskets for all my containers, have rocks in every nook and cranny, and my curtain rods are branches from trees. Just go as far as you are comfortable, while utilizing the elements of the earth as much as possible. I always say, if I cannot live totally outside, then the outside will have to come inside! You will find a level of comfort and way to have nature inside your home that suits you the best. Even having lots of plants can connect your inside to the outside.

- We can lie upon the earth and soak up the higher realms. These harmonious and connected energies will absolutely seep into your body as you simply lie upon her surface. When I used to live in the mountains of Northeastern Arizona, many days I would find a beautiful spot by the river and just be, while lying flat on my back. Now in the red rocks of New Mexico, I can have this same experience while lying upon a rock or at the foot of some falls. Lying on a rock can be truly awesome, as the denser energy of rocks is able to hold many of the earth's secrets. The ancients knew this, as this is why they built utilizing rock formations as much as possible. And when in the stillness of the ancient sites, the ancient ones usually "come out" of hiding and keep me company. These are some of my favorite past times, as the nature spirits and otherwise quiet and invisible realms always come out to join me. It truly places me in another world at the same time that these higher energies are infusing into my body. And it is absolutely free! Going out into your backyard and lying upon the grass can work just as well. You will find yourself connecting to a very new reality.

- We can eat organic as much as possible, and use organic products as well. These are more purified aspects of the earth and assist in keeping us in alignment with her bounty. We are all made up of the same thing, and pristine is the key, as this is what the ascension process is creating within us...purification! As we begin to vibrate higher, we will no longer need to consciously choose specific foods, as the higher vibrations within everything we eat, will naturally match up with our higher vibrational selves, and we will then naturally utilize whatever we need from whatever we eat. Any lower vibrating aspects of foods we consume will simply fall away from us, without ever making a connection. So in this way, as we arrive at higher levels of vibration within ourselves, we can eventually eat whatever feels right or sounds good.

- We can hand-make things as an outlet for our creativity...woodworking, painting, weaving, sewing, making pottery, and even preparing as much of our own food as possible from the purest forms of nature and the animal kingdom. These practices are more time consuming, but as we evolve into a simpler life-style, they fit right in and are very rewarding as well. They just plain *feel good.*

- If you cannot build your own natural home (they are surprisingly inexpensive, and you can start small and add on), you can adjust and modify your current home. The internet has a wealth of information about passive solar options (water heaters and more), wind and solar power, solar greenhouse design, rainwater harvesting, and even how to build a cold frame for growing your own garden year-round. With the incentive-based rebates available, federal and state tax credits, new lower cost and more efficient solar products, a well as options such as the sale of electricity back to the utility, and even carbon credits and green tag trading, living off-grid and in alignment with the earth is becoming more beneficial than ever.

There are many wonderful books out there as well. Even re-plastering the interior or exterior of your home with natural earth plasters can add an earthen element, or adding natural wooden beams, for instance. And in addition, living in a home surrounded by something created by ourselves, makes us feel great and aligns us with our own energy too!

- Join a food co-op or community garden if you cannot grow your own organic. There are many out there, and those in our own community always seem to know about them. My neighbors and I trade produce, and it's free.

- As we evolve more fully, we will come to know that the earth holds the keys to much. In this way, we will utilize her bounty by growing our own foods, using the sun to heat our homes, utilizing the energies the planets and planetary alignments bring to support us in our daily lives, and simply allowing ourselves to align with and accept the earth and all that she brings.

Not Taking Things Personally

Several years ago I was in a group setting where we were practicing EFT (Emotional Freedom Technique). EFT is a healing and energy balancing modality which stems from the core belief that *"The cause of all negative emotions is a disruption in the body's energy system."* And *"Our unresolved negative emotions are major contributors to most physical pains and diseases."* (For more information kindly visit http://www.emofree.com.) Through a process of tapping on the meridian points of the body, these energy disruptions or blockages can then be released and re-framed.

When I first began experiencing the discomfort of the higher energies hitting my blocked energy spots from toddler rapes, abuse, and much life trauma, this process was greatly helpful in the beginning stages. (Please note that as we progress through the ascension process, many kinds of healing only serve to take us back into spaces where we are no longer vibrating, and thus, healing is no longer needed and is even detrimental. Also, we eventually see that nothing needs to be "fixed" or is wrong once we reach a certain vibration. Our new little ones receiving vaccinations is another example of energies that are totally out of alignment and way too much of a stretch. The vaccinations contain very low level energy and this energy is extremely uncomfortable to these new and higher vibrating babies...and the vaccinations exist in another reality altogether! I am not suggesting or telling anyone what to do here, in this regard. My grandchildren still receive vaccinations, as my daughter feels that this is the right thing.

It is always best to go with what feels right to you at the time, as this will place you in alignment with yourself.)

While we were tapping away one evening, something suddenly became vibrantly clear. One of the many wonderful things about EFT, is that is serves to give a person the clear and "real" version of things (without the human mis-perceptions and density). What became so blatantly obvious was that what holds us back so many times, is the human pattern of taking things personally. This is because we tend to view things from our ego stance, or dis-connect stance, or rather, through the filter of our blocked energy. We think that everything is about *us*.

"How can we not take things personally, when we only attract what we are vibrating in the first place?" you may wonder. What holds true for all of creation, or how creating works, is that we create from both sides. For example: Most of you who are reading this, realize that we are most certainly going through a spiritual evolutionary process while here in form. What created this process, and why did it begin in the first place? It is being fueled from the outside *and* from the inside. Our positioning in the universe, and the positioning of the planets, is creating it on the outside.

So are the solar flares, and basically all of the cosmos. This is resulting in a raising of our vibration. At the same time, we as human beings, and all the non-physical beings, are summoning this process from the inside. So then, everything is happening at once...culminating in one big creation that meets in a portal of creation in the middle.

Did the chicken lay the egg, or did the egg lay the chicken? Which came first? In all of creation, everything happens at once when vibrations reach a certain level of frequency. It is then that manifestation occurs when things culminate through like energies attracting like energies. Similar to always having everything we need, the pieces come together more easily when there is less density. So then, do we attract our experiences, or do our experiences attract us? And how does this relate to not taking things personally?

As we vibrate higher and higher, we shed off our density, or the lower vibrating aspects of ourselves. Higher and lower energies cannot exist in the same space, and we are now residing in a higher realm. We only react to things if they trigger something within us that is a match in vibration. As we begin to vibrate higher, we then begin to embody higher ways of *being*, and not reacting to the outside environment is one of these ways of being. Just like all of the nature kingdom, we eventually come to a place where we simply *are*. The more purified version of ourselves is composed of our special gifts and talents, our connection to Source, and not much else. In this way, we can be shining our brightest light the majority of the time. Everything else belongs to someone or something else.

There are times when we must visit the lower vibrating aspects of reality, as all of the earth is not yet in the same space of vibration and evolution. As always, we can spend time in the denser vibrations, but not for very long, as it is just too unpleasant and at times intolerable. This is the way it was intended. One way to "survive" while dropping down and visiting the lower vibrations is to simply shine our light as brightly as we can. This involves not taking things personally, or reacting to and becoming involved with the dramas that may be occurring. When we interact or respond to these lower vibrating dramas, we then become a part of them ourselves, and only serve to fuel and support them. In addition, reacting to any lower vibrating dramas (or creations) activates them within us as well (just as receiving certain types of healing does). Eventually, the energies that we have not yet released or balanced within us, simply become dormant. So when we are in a higher vibrating reality, they do not become activated; similar to the process of natural selection.

By simply being who we are at our highest levels, just like a flower would do, for instance, we are then able to raise the vibration we are in, as well as maintaining our own. Staying centered with who we truly are, while maintaining a connection to Source, is the best way to survive any visits to the denser realities. Most things on the outside eventually do not ever belong to us....period.

When we attract situations in our lives that create an emotional response, or charge, this is because we have a corresponding energy pattern that is connected to our disconnect or ego selves. As we begin to evolve, we can still attract situations or see them unfolding around us, but if we have no particular feelings or emotions about them, then we are free and clear to be who we are at the highest levels. Not taking things personally is one way to do this. Energies we encounter are not always about *us*. This is one of the reasons I love writing the energy alerts. The energy alerts serve to show us that we are all one, having the same experience. In this way, we need not take things personally.

When we all experience the same thing at the same time, we come to know then, that we have not done anything wrong, are not attracting a bad experience because we have an "issue," and everything is as it should be. We are just vibrating higher and going through the same stages of ascension at the same time. All is in perfect order, as this is what we came to do.

 ## Staying In Alignment With Not Taking Things Personally

There are two ways that I have found helpful to stay connected to the higher realms or vibrations when we encounter a situation that stirs an unpleasant reaction in us.

1.   Suppose someone arrives in your reality that is embodying an energy that you find annoying or unpleasant. They seem to become a bur under your saddle, so to speak, and you find that you would prefer to avoid them. In this case, it can be helpful to do this: Ask yourself what it is about their energy that defines what is bothering you. What is it about? Then identify that energy within yourself. This is no new news here, and no new process.

After you identify what it is that their particularly bothersome energy is about, then you have the opportunity to adjust that energy within yourself. When particular individuals enter our spaces with bothersome energy, it is almost always because it is now time for a particular adjustment within ourselves to occur. This is why it is coming to our attention.

If you cannot identify that particular energy within yourself (and remember, it may be an energy that you *could* embody under certain circumstances, or an energy that you *do* embody, but in a different way and in a different arena, so it may be hard to recognize), then know that it is then an energy that you may have a strong reaction to or judgment about, so you would never consciously want to embody it.

In this case, you are being asked to be *more* of that energy, but probably in a more healthy and balanced way. This particular energy is just being shown to you in an exaggerated way so that you will not miss it. We may think that *no-one* should ever embody this energy, and certainly then, not us! We have strong reactions to certain energies because we think they are very wrong and not of the highest order, but when this is the case, what is really occurring is that we are not right and the other is not wrong. In time, if we are open and willing, we always find that we were overly exaggerated in our judgment, and these seemingly horrible energies are actually OK if they are used appropriately (in other words, not to such a strong and exaggerated degree.) For some reason specific to us, we believe that these unpleasant energies are absolutely not acceptable, and so we would *never* embody them ourselves! So then, we need to embody them ourselves, and find their gifts and benefits, in order to diffuse and neutralize these reactions we are having. We need to acknowledge their gifts and benefits, and embrace them and become them in order to become whole. Thus, we need not take this personally, as energy is simply doing what energy does.

As we evolve higher and higher, we begin to experience less of number 1, and more of number 2.

2. We eventually come to a space of being, where we are aware that a specific energy is in our space,

but we have no reaction to it, except that it is unpleasant and it feels as though it belongs somewhere other than where we are. It can almost feel repulsive. We can easily see what it is about, and intuitively we know that we have already been there ourselves, understand this energy, and know we no longer embody it. It may even feel as though it lives in a land far away...a land where we have not lived for a very long time. In this case, we are then able to give love and understanding to the individual who is embodying this energy, and thus, we do not take it personally.

Even though we have now evolved out of many lower vibrating energy patterns, they can still feel fairly uncomfortable to be around. When we encounter them, we have a strong desire to be somewhere else. This is because *higher vibrating energies cannot exist in the same space as lower vibrating energies.* Knowing who we are at the highest levels, staying in that space, and shining our lights while being connected to Source while not taking things personally, is a good way to spend the limited amount of time we may find ourselves residing in the lower vibrating realities. Things are only about us if we choose to take them personally.

Creating in the Higher Realms

Residing in a new higher vibration calls for a regular set of guidelines for creating. Being that the higher realms energies are much more refined and clear than 3D reality energies, creating can get to be great fun indeed.

There are several repetitive themes that become ever evident as we begin creating in this New World of a higher vibrating reality, and many of them are not new to us:

- We always have everything we need (as defined and explained previously).
- Like energies attract like energies much more frequently and powerfully in a higher vibrating reality (as there is less density). In addition, we create what we *truly are* (or our pure and authentic selves) as we vibrate higher, vs. creating more of our mis-perceptions and/or "issues" when

we embodied a lower vibration.....in other words, things get better because we are better.

- A space of letting go or detachment is needed when creating.
- We can now create at much quicker speeds.
- We are now running the show with much less interference; there-for many of the old roadblocks from the denser 3D reality are gone.
- We are now creating at soul levels, like never before.
- Creating is much easier when we create higher vibrational things, as we are now much more of a match for them.
- In the higher realms, we create much more as a whole.
- In the higher realms, we create more in alignment with our purpose and geographical home on Earth.

Even with the general principles above, there is a foundation and a theme that runs through all the aspects of creating at the beginning levels of the dimensional hierarchy ...and this is the theme of creating *very deliberately* and *consciously*. As we progress further along with our spiritual evolutionary process, we become less and less concerned with creating than with simply *being* ...experiencing states of love, joy, gratitude, and being in the moment. Creating then goes to a very new and different level. Consciously creating then becomes fairly moot.

In the beginning stages of our evolutionary path then, we find that we are suddenly more aware of:

Conscious Creating

It is very common before a big leap in dimensional residency to find ourselves being trained or guided into being *very comfortable asking for what we want*. We usually receive this training or guidance through personal experiences and through strong messages. This is what we need to "get" if we are going to be residing at the beginning levels of this new and higher vibrating reality. Conscious creating then, requires that we be very comfortable asking for what we want. It is also about claiming our power.

As we progress further along on our spiritual paths, through suffering and various other wearing away experiences that the ascension process creates, we begin to become more and more aware of what it is that we really and truly want. So then, what we really and truly want can change as we progress. This is because our "ego" selves, or the aspects of us that thought they were in charge or were tuned into a different frequency and reality, begin to slowly disappear with each new stage of ascension.

How is this special "training" or fine tuning that is encouraging us to be comfortable asking for what we want, manifesting in our lives, and why is it a necessary part of our spiritual evolutionary process?

The First Stage....Morphing Into Conscious Creators

As we begin to evolve and "remember," we begin to learn (or re-learn) what energy is all about. We remember and very deeply know that everything in the universe is comprised of energy, and thus, energy is the root or core of every creation. The earth was designed to be a playground for experiencing and creating. Therefore, in order to be in alignment with being on the earth, creating is a key aspect of our residency here. This is one of the reasons why creating is such a hot topic, as creating is a key component of being in physical form, and of utilizing the energy of Source. Many of you reading this have created planets, their life systems, other universes, and much more. Playing with and understanding how to utilize energy then, becomes much more conscious as we evolve.

As we evolve beyond experiencing life as a cause and effect experience from *unconscious* creating, where we possess much more of a victim stance with our experiences, creating, then, can be much more fun. In the old 3D reality, we were very cut off and removed from the higher energies we are now currently residing in. This situation caused memory loss, confusion, and much more of a disconnection from Source and from our soul energy. Denser energy creates blockages, interference, lack of memory regarding Source related connections and perceptions, and basically, an inability to "see" or to remember.

If we are such highly evolved souls, and we absolutely are, why then did we forget everything, including how to utilize our true powers of creation when we first arrived in our current incarnation? Why did we suffer and struggle so? Why weren't we born with the wisdom and knowledge of creating with ease?

When many of us arrived here on the earth this time around, we were basically done with our evolutionary process. We had experienced all that we could through infusing our soul energy into many different forms. We had expanded as far as was possible. As described in earlier sections of this book, we were now ready to move on and experience an entirely new universe. We decided then, to wrap things up here, complete what we had originally created, and set up a new planet Earth...a new planet Earth in a very pristine condition, so that others could then experience her as she was originally created (and then some)...as a playground for creating and experiencing energy through form.

We arrived then, as conduits and highly evolved entities for the purpose of releasing, letting go, and purifying all the old denser energies of each and every experience we had had in the cosmos... through ourselves. It was through ourselves that we were successful in completing the first phase of this process. Remember, we infused our soul energy everywhere. So then, we were everything. This process was a painful one indeed, and even more so because we were still residing in the lower frequencies and could not then, remember what we were actually doing. Almost each and every ancient being of light currently residing here had chosen to experience forms of darkness in our early years, so that we could transmute these energies. This is why so many are attracted to the healing arena and may not consciously know why. It is because they want to transmute these energies so that we can move forward into the light.

Because of this process, at times we thought we were suffering and perhaps even being punished. It is ironic to a degree, that after we purified and released so much, we were then able to raise the vibration of the planet as a whole, as well as ourselves (as we are everything), and then we could remember much more easily...but it was after the fact! Thank goodness at some level we had some degree of trust in Source, and that our souls were navigating our direction. Trust involves a deep faith with no evidence, explanation, or proof...and trust is what can always serve to carry us through rocky and confusing times if we allow it to. Our souls know what they are doing, and this inner knowing, although often consciously forgotten, is what continues to carry us through. The higher we evolve, the less we need trust. So trust, then, will become another obsolete word. The more we evolve, the more we connect to and become our souls, and our souls know *everything*.

So now that we are residing in a higher vibrating reality, because we were successful with our first mission of purification and evolution, we can then begin creating much more consciously, as this is a new way of being for us now. Watch as conscious creating now becomes a reality within the mainstream. Watch as conscious creating is embraced by many as never before. Very soon, it will become a natural and accepted way of being, and many of us will be the instrumental teachers of making this the New Reality.

As evolution is occurring *through* us, and will continue on for some time as we are taking everyone and everything with us, we really need to get it down correctly (or in its most purified form). We need to learn to be masters at it. As we are the teachers, way-showers, and the ones who embody these new ways, it is vitally important then, that we really know what we are doing in regard to creating.

So then, we have been having experiences and receiving messages which are encouraging and supporting us in being very comfortable in asking for what we want, as this is a key component in conscious creating. How then, has this way of asking for what we want been manifesting in our lives, and how can we benefit the greatest from these messages and experiences?

Being Aligned and Fine Tuned Into Conscious Creators

A large part of being a conscious creator involves being comfortable with asking and knowing what we want, and expecting that what we want will and *should* occur, with no doubts, insecurities, or fears. Anything within us that is not in alignment with being comfortable asking for what we want is now being tweaked so that it *will* be in alignment. How then, are we experiencing this "tweaking?"

We are aligning and adjusting our energy to the center for optimum balance, or in other words, to the space of stillness. If you are one who is weak in asking for what you want (and many of us are), you will have experiences and messages which will support you in being more *forthcoming*, assertive, or outward moving with your energy instead of being very laid back or having a "doormat" energy. If you are one who is usually more demanding and domineering (and there are plenty of us that are this way as well), you will then have experiences and messages that will support you in standing back and *allowing* in regard to your energy. If you are very comfortable stating what you want and expecting it to arrive, without violating the needs of others or without the opposing energy of placing the needs of others ahead of yours, you will not need any tweaking at all.

Those of us who are opposed to what we interpret as "dominance" as a way of being and running one's energy, will most likely need tweaking in regard to becoming more dominant ourselves. We will find ourselves attracting and having judgment about people and experiences in our lives that are running a "take over" or "want everything their way" energy. These individuals appear to us to want everything the way they want it, with no regard to those around them. They "appear" to be unable to work as a team. We, on the other hand, believe we are very considerate of others needs and wants, and are the right ones, of course, but most likely by over-accommodating others. There is an imbalance here that is trying to be corrected, and it will continue on until we learn to run our energy more like what we are attracting.

Those of us who continually attract passive people into our lives who appear to us to be unable to stand up for what they want, or seem to be holding back their energy most of the time, are most likely ready to become more like them, or more "passive." Even though they may frustrate us at times, and we just want to shake them and say "speak up!" they are serving their purpose. We are being encouraged to be more allowing, to step back and not fill up the space with so much of our own desires and forceful energy.

Extreme energies usually attract other extreme energies, both vibrating with the perfect opposing vibration in equal amounts of extremism. In other words, because the universe naturally attempts to create balance, extreme energies always attract opposing energies which carry the same amount of imbalance, and which carry the same "theme."

And there is yet a third, but much easier to digest scenario as well. We can also attract others and experiences into our space that *match* our imbalance in asking for what we want, as they are just like us. These individuals serve to greatly highlight how we are ourselves vibrating, and we can then truly see what we look like and where we need to make an adjustment. These types of situations are not nearly as challenging, as we understand why these individuals are behaving as they are (because they are like us!). None-the-less, there are many variations and levels of imbalance....all serving to illuminate who we are and how we are running our own energy.

We run our energy the way we do because we feel we are absolutely doing the right, best, and highest vibrating thing. We truly believe that our way is the best way, and because of this, others may appear to be the villains in our scenario. No one is either right or wrong. There is a healthy way to run our energy in regard to asking for what we want, and if we can embrace these experiences and messages which we are receiving, through understanding that the seemingly opposing viewpoint is not so bad (when it is adjusted to an appropriate and balanced way), we can make some great progress.

There is a global scenario presenting itself in strengthening a healthy way of being in regard to asking for what we want. The occurrences in Africa are supporting us in standing up to what we will no longer tolerate. We are creating a very New World, and genocide and other atrocities against human beings do not fit in with a higher vibrating reality. So then, these situations are getting much more intense in order to offer the planet an opportunity to speak out and take action to stop these old 3D manifestations of lower vibrating energy. We are then being supported in asking for what we want and in accepting nothing less. We are being supported by the inhabitants of Africa who are experiencing these atrocities. These incredible souls are shining their lights, utilizing their soul energy for the purpose of illuminating what needs to change. These are brave and selfless souls, serving the planet as they support the whole, as they encourage us to create a planet where these things can no longer exist. Things will get as bad as they need to in order to attract the attention needed, so that enough of us will stand up and demand what we want and demand what we require a higher vibrating planet to look like.

In the beginning stages of ascension, we are learning and being supported in taking the reigns now in regard to creating....because in the higher realms we are no longer victims of *unconscious* creating. And as we know what we would like the New World to look like, and have known for a very long time, we are now at an evolutionary pivotal point to begin creating it by asking for and demanding what we want.

So then, one of the first stages in being conscious creators is being comfortable asking for what we want. Through this process, any energies relating to self-worth, lack of confidence and deservability, and the like, are processed and released as well. In this regard, the universe is supporting us in balancing our energies so that we will begin to vibrate in this way very naturally. If we are unbalanced in any way, we will undoubtedly know it by what we find ourselves attracting and by the experiences we are having. It can be easy to fall back into old grooves of past experience where darkness ruled the roost and we had little power. But as the tide begins to change, we must be ready to change with it.

After we experience and have embodied this evolutionary stage, we then move into another. We do not think about creating as much, as all our needs are always met, we feel very removed from the old reality, and we are then moved more fully into a space of being, enjoying, experiencing, and of service to humanity. We have gotten outside of ourselves.

The Old Scenario of Creating...Bye Bye!

It seems that all many of us have known up until recent times relates to having life and life circumstances run us, instead of vice versa. In the old 3D reality, each and every thing seemed to mysteriously arrive on its own, and we spent much time then, putting out fires, solving dilemmas, and just trying to survive. We barely had time to smell the roses, enjoy life, be in our creativity, and have even one moment to become clear about what we wanted for ourselves...not to mention our illusions of having to create solely with money or having to survive in a monetary based controlled society!

The New Reality is nothing like this. One reason is because much of the density is now gone. In the old 3D world, we experienced many roadblocks to creating. We had to navigate around a lot of denser energy, and much of this energy simply no longer exists.

So then, residing in a new and higher vibration brings some truly wonderful things in regard to creating. Much is different...this world and reality is fresh and new...we can begin to be in what appears to be Heaven at last.

Guidelines for Creating in the Higher Realms

- *Like energies attract like energies much more frequently and powerfully in a higher vibrating reality (as there is less density). Therefore, we create what we are.*

One day several years ago, I was out on the Hopi Reservation at Oraibi. From the top of the mesa, one could clearly see for miles. 90 miles off in the distance were the San Francisco Peaks near Flagstaff. In between was virtually nothing in regard to population or physical structures. Sitting there that day, it was easy to go back in time, to another world of long ago; two power spots connected with virtually nothing in between them. The same scenario is true for the ancients. In the area where I once lived in the mountains Northeastern Arizona and where I now live in New Mexico, this way of existence was the same. During the ancient times when the energies were still pristine and pure (the *very* beginning of the ancient times), each pueblo or ancient power spot was connected to another, with not much of anything in between. And each and every one of these ancient sites or places of community carried a very specific theme. Each and every theme or purpose was very unique as they connected to each other, with nothing in between, thus creating a whole.

And this is how it is in the higher vibrating realities. With less and less density present, there are then more and more spaces in between realities or higher vibrating manifestations. Thus, this scenario allows for like energies to attract like energies much more frequently and powerfully.

After so much clearing and releasing of the lower vibrating energies of the 3D reality, what remains is a more fine tuned and higher vibrating human, planet, and reality. Much of the density which filled in the gaps is gone....higher vibrating energy, then, is attracting other higher vibrating energy.

And being that this density is now much more absent, attracting higher vibrating energies and experiences is happening much more frequently and with much more ease. How awesome it is indeed!

Yes, we attract what we are vibrating . What we *are*, is what will surround us. What we are *being*, is what will surround us. When what we are and what we are being involves being in the moment and being present with where we currently are, then we are in alignment. If we are continually striving to have more, or are focusing on where we want to be other than where we are, we will then be nowhere. We can only create from a space of being in alignment with where we currently are. This involves being still and being present, otherwise Source cannot find us as we are a continual moving target and in standing in our own way as well. This way of being holds true for our store-fronts too. We need to be *found* so that money can know where it needs to go...it needs a target. (This will be explained much more fully in the section *Setting Up Our Store-Fronts* further on in this book.)

Because we have cleared and released so much since the year 2000, we are now poised to surround ourselves with much in the way of a higher vibrating reality. We have truly earned it! And with less density present, we no longer have to navigate around roadblocks, delays, and resistances that were present in the 3D world.

- *A space of letting go or detachment is needed when creating.*

No new news here. When we place a choke hold on anything, it cannot breathe. The energy cannot move and nothing can then arrive for us. As mentioned above, if we spend too much time wishing, wanting, and focusing on what we desire, we will not be in the present moment. We will not be in alignment with where we currently are. No portal or vortex can then be created, and this is needed for creation. Portals and vortexes are created when there are alignments. And alignments arrive when things are still and present, all in the same space.

One great way to create very easily is to simply daydream about something that is desired. A daydreaming state of mind places us in the space of letting go, or basically a no choke hold space. The daydreaming space lets go of attachment energy as well. Having a desire rolling around in the back of our minds with no agenda or "have to have it" energy attached to it will almost always bring it to us, unless we evolve out of that creation before it arrives! This state is easy to achieve if we can be happy and grateful for the space we are currently in. And as most of us know, gratitude brings with it many more things to be grateful for....like a snowball effect, what we are being or vibrating is what will surround us.

Knowing we always have everything that we need places us in alignment with this space as well. Knowing we have everything that we need, places us in the present moment, and that is where creation occurs. The space in between thoughts in a meditation, gazing at a beautiful sunset, stopping to smell the roses and appreciate all the simplicity that surrounds us each and every day, and noticing what is right in front of us and always has been, will *always* put us in a space for creating anything and everything. It is because we are truly happy and enjoying where we are, that we then receive more.....and it is always when we do not care anymore that we get what we once wanted!

- *We can now create at much quicker speeds.*

Energy vibrates faster in the higher realms. And in this regard, we are now able to create much more quickly, as we are now residing in a higher and faster vibrating reality. Because of this phenomenon, our manifestations are arriving much quicker that we are accustomed to. At times, it may seem that there is less time in any given day, and part of this is because we are creating and manifesting much faster. And many times, our manifestations will begin arriving, but we are evolving so quickly within, that they are no longer a match for who we are! But this is the beauty of manifesting. We can create fresh and new at any given moment. And if we have evolved beyond our prior desires, we can then create something totally new that fits us oh so much better. It seems that we need only have a casual thought about something, and it shows up at our doorstep in record time. (And it is the "casual" thought that brings it to us in the first place!)

For bigger and more substantial creations, or rather creations that involve an entirely new space for ourselves that will affect much in our lives (a new geographical area, new career, new relationship, etc.), the manifestation time is greater. There are several reasons for this. When we strive to create the bigger manifestations for ourselves, we are usually much more attached to them and their outcome, and this state of being serves to slow things up a bit more. Also, there are many more things that need to be in alignment with bigger manifestations.

There are also times when we cannot move forward into certain situations, as the higher we vibrate, the more that we create as a whole. We have to wait for enough of the masses to catch up to where we are. We are then able to move forward when everyone else is on board. Remember, we are all one at certain levels, and are here to create a higher vibrating planet as a whole before we can move on to a very new and different reality in another universe. In this way, we are holding the space for those who will come after us before we can then move on.

- *We are now running the show with much less interference; therefore many of the old roadblocks are gone.*

Basically, much of the interfering darkness is finally gone (especially if you choose to believe this and to focus on positive and higher vibrating things). This darkness or denser energy could really wreak havoc in our lives. It created doubts, negative thinking, roadblocks, and even a world where there was a dark force running the show in the physical reality of the masses. These energies have now lost their foothold...the light has risen to a level where it is now the predominating force here on the planet. Continuing to focus on these energies which no longer have a foot-hold, will only place you in alignment with them.

There are many levels of so-called darkness. Some might say that they are personally being "attacked" by the dark forces as these individuals hold so much light, and so forth. A higher version or interpretation which is very evident to me, is that all darkness comes from within us. As it is released and purged through the ascension process, it appears to be gaining, but it is only really leaving....and that is why we see it so much more. I don't believe as some do, that we are so incredibly awesome that we are totally light filled and darkness then tries to sabotage us. I do believe we are incredibly awesome, but the darkness we experience can only be present if we have it within ourselves, or if we have a corresponding hook or charge that gives it power...or even if we focus upon it.

In addition, when we are experiencing a substantial purging, as we do many times during this monumental process, we begin creating through the filter of the darkness that we are releasing. Thus, we experience and create dark scenarios, and may feel that we are being sabotaged or attacked, when all that is really occurring is that we are creating through these filters of the denser energies that are leaving. There was never really any such thing as darkness or the boogie man, or even Satan. It is always simply us...just as our spirit guides or even Archangel Michael are all simply aspects of ourselves which we prefer to place outside of ourselves.

Enough said. Basically, there is incredibly less darkness than ever before, so we are now able to move forward with much less resistance.

- *We are now creating at soul levels, like never before.*

What does creating at soul levels mean?

Very naturally, we connect with things that vibrate the way that we do (unless it is a soul connection for a higher purpose). Some call this the Law of Attraction, or in other words, like energies attracting like energies.

If ever I am concerned or feeling not quite right about an energy alert, sure enough I will immediately receive an email that complains about the exact aspects of the energy alert that had been troubling me. Here in the Southwest, hot summers are a regular event ....and rattlesnakes come right along with them. With various reports of rattlesnake run-ins from my neighbors my first summer here in New Mexico, I began to become concerned about my own surroundings and started to focus on fears about them. Thus, I decided to check out my back porch and sure enough, a rattler was lounging around within a few feet of my door (I had invited him with my energy). After speaking with the rattlesnake soul energy, gaining an understanding of their energy, and thus diffusing my fears, I never encountered another one...on a trail or in my yard, even though many others had very differing experiences. I now absolutely adore rattlesnakes!

But creating at soul levels goes far beyond and vibrates much higher than creating with like energies attracting like energies. Creating at soul levels involves having experiences and attracting things which are not in our conscious minds, but which are all about our soul's purposes and intentions. We are creating at soul levels when we at times experience miracles, or things that do not seem to match the level where we are vibrating. In regard to attracting individuals into our lives, we can attract people to us who are far more spiritually and emotionally healthy than we are, and we can also attract individuals to us who still have great unresolved issues (when we have made great progress in clearing and balancing our own related issues).

Souls come together to help one another, even if for no other reason and if this union and support absolutely makes no plausible sense. At soul levels, there is no lower vibrating energy, and thus, we come into contact with one another from a much higher level....a level where we are brothers and sisters and where our denser energies of "issues" and unpleasant behavior do not exist. In this way, it is expected that we overlook these lower vibrating energies in order to complete a project we came to complete or to simply assist one another when assistance and support is vitally needed. These types of soul level unions are usually very brief unless the soul's energies also match at lower levels as well.

In geographical communities where "lightworkers" and those spiritually inclined tend to congregate, there can at times seem to be much bickering, clashing, and gossiping present. This is because the denser energy of "issues" and egos is still very present. Many are not yet ready to congregate at higher levels. So then, even though at times we may resist others at human levels, when something is very important to our progress or soul plan, we will be thrown together with a soul companion, even if it does not seem to make sense or remotely follow the lower level experience of like energies attracting like energies. We can be separated from companions at soul levels just as well. This usually occurs when one soul is choosing at a soul level to support another's next step, soul plan, or purpose, and will then set that soul free.

Soul level creation always takes precedence over personal or human level creation. It overrides all creation each and every time. It also overrides the lower level of like energies attracting like energies. In other words, in the higher realms, the energies are less dense and the attractions and unions then become more about soul level experiences. Thus, the purpose of unions is no longer about lower vibrating "issues attracting issues" for the old 3D purpose of balancing and clearing.

What are some indicators of soul level creation?

Things will come out of your mouth and you will wonder who said them. Things will occur in your life that do not feel like they were your idea at all. You may have experiences that force you to greatly bump up your soul growth, as you may not be ready yet for the soul plan that is arriving for you none-the-less. You may be forced to proceed forward with a geographical move, a relationship, or some kind of work that you do not feel you are ready for. At the level of soul creation, everything is orchestrated for us and extremely quickly. This is because it is now time at higher levels. When the frequencies on the planet reach a certain level of vibration and evolutionary growth, the new unfolds as never before. Our programming from eons past kicks in and away we go. Our plan before birth is now ready for hatching.

So then, we are not always consciously and emotionally in alignment with our soul plan, but when it is time on the planet, our soul plan arrives none-the-less. And even though we may resist it, as we may feel that we know best, our souls *always* know best as they are vibrating the highest. There are times as well when we are very ready, but the frequencies have not yet reached a certain level and all the conditions on the outside have not yet been met. Then we must wait.

If you are one who has had a severe physical malady that has forced you to adjust the way you run your energy, or experienced something life changing that you did not think was your idea, you are most likely having these kinds of experiences because your soul is dictating them. Because our souls vibrate higher than our human selves, and being that we are now in higher vibrating energy, we are having more and more soul level experiences. The ascension process brings us closer and closer to our conscious soul level selves. Our souls know more than we do and are following a higher level plan!

- *Creating is much easier when we create higher vibrational things.*

Because we are now residing in the higher realms, creating is much easier when we match (or are in alignment with) the vibration we are now residing in. Trying to create something that matches a lower vibrating frequency, or that is of a 3D nature, is much more difficult as the older systems and ways of being no longer fit where we are currently residing. There is simply too much of a stretch now as the lower and denser vibrations are further beneath us.

This is why so many of us have lost our jobs and cannot seem to find replacements. This is why we are being yanked out of the mainstream in so many ways, as the mainstream vibrates so much lower than the new and higher vibrations within us. We are simply no longer a match anymore. And again, this has always been one of the challenges of the ascension process; we continually vibrate higher than our prior surroundings, or what has been created before, and thus we feel we have no sense of place. (Within the sections about soul purpose and our store-fronts further along in this book, you will be guided into ways of staying in alignment and flourishing when much else is falling around you....so hang in there just a bit longer!)

There have also been times in our spiritual evolutionary process where we have tried to create something that comes from more of an ego stance or from a place that we are very soon going to be out of. We just cannot seem to get anywhere. It is as if nothing will happen for us, and we may feel that we have no power at all. This phase I have come to label as the "*stop sign* energy phase." We are usually in the midst of one of the shifts when this occurs.

During these shifts, we find that we loose yet another piece of who we thought we were, or a part of us that was very in charge of what we thought we wanted. We used to be so excited about creating this particular thing, or dream, and then suddenly we may wonder whom that dream or desire actually belonged to in the first place! When we eventually move out of the space of our "old" selves (during the shifting) we usually find that we did not really want to create that particular thing in the first place. We may also find that what we *now* want to create comes from a much higher place within us. It is now much more of a match to whom we currently are. And it is much more of a match then, to the higher realms or higher vibrations. So in this way, even though we may feel powerless and frustrated for a time, we are eventually oh so grateful that we were unable to create what we thought we wanted, as we would have had to create something entirely different before we even had a chance to enjoy our old desire!

What are some higher vibrational creations that never seemingly change or never seem to leave us as we journey though this change provoking ascension process?

Anything that is in alignment with our soul purpose, or basically our own special gifts and talents and why we are here (again, there will be assists in identifying your soul purpose further along in this book);

Anything that places us in alignment with the earth, as she is our ascension vehicle;

Anything that places us in a creative arena most of the time, as creativity is the mainstay of higher vibrational living;

Anything that supports what is deeply within us...so if we created something that makes us feel good from an external source, this would only be a temporary fix;

Anything that serves humanity, or the whole. And this brings us to the next category...

- *In the higher realms, we create much more as a whole.*

In the higher realms, we know that we are all one. We know that what we choose to create affects each and every one of us. We are ever mindful then, of how our actions and creations affect others, as we are very aware of our brothers and sisters and love them dearly.

We are also very much on the same page. We share the same visions, and this places us in alignment with each other. In this regard, the energies of creation are much more powerful as we are all going in the same direction and in a much more conscious way.

In the old 3D reality, we were all going in the same direction as well, but it might not have appeared this way. This was because at human levels, individuals were at times exhibiting behaviors and situations were presenting themselves in ways that would encourage a change in those involved with them. So there was always support at a higher soul level, even though our human selves were not aware of it. For example, darkness exists to spur us on to create something new, or to create within us who we originally intended to be. So although it may appear and feel as if there is a great contrast or chasm between ourselves and those who appear to be abusing us or making our journey uncomfortable, these souls are usually only supporting us at soul levels. They are very on track with our path and supporting us in getting there through their poking, nudging, and "making us miserable" behavior. Thus, at higher levels there is really no such thing as darkness.

I remember a time when I relocated from the Southwest to North Carolina. I was devastated that my beloved male companion would not come with me, or even come for a visit. I felt totally abandoned by him. While being miserable about this one day, and in a state of great sorrow and confusion, I suddenly had a higher level vision. There he was, straddling the space between himself and me. At soul levels, he was doing a wonderful job of encouraging me to stand on my own two feet, connect to my own power, and to learn to be very comfortable on my own. After I had this vision, I then felt much better as I knew that I was deeply loved and that all was in divine and perfect order. We still remained close friends for many years after that.

Another typical scenario that I have seen repeatedly is when one soul leaves another. The "left" soul feels abandoned, ashamed, loses trust, and may even feel a loss of self worth. What is actually occurring here is the total opposite. The soul who has left, has done so at a soul level because of a great love for the other soul. The "abandoned" soul was left because he/she was ever so ready to move on with their expansion and soul plan and the other soul was holding him/her back. So even though one may feel as if they are not worth much, they are actually doing so well, that they need to move on and would not do so on their own.

In the higher realms, we are very aware of what we are doing. We are much more connected to the higher ways, know what they are, and are then very consciously creating a world and relationships that are of a higher level. Much of the denser illusions are gone, and we are then able to consciously create as a whole. We want what is the best for all of us, and everyone is considered.

In the higher realms, polarity greatly diminishes. We are able to see through the din or the density, and always *know* what another's journey is really about, at a much more conscious level. In this regard, we no longer need polarity, and it cannot really exist in a higher vibrating reality anyway.

So then, we are all always going in the same direction, supporting each other and the whole, but in the higher realms we are much more aware of it, as we are able to see things from a much higher perspective as we are now residing in a much higher vibration. I remember when I wrote an energy alert in 2004 when George W. Bush had just been re-elected. I wrote of the beauty of his soul, as he very much needed to be President of the US for a while longer, as he was succeeding beautifully in *being* what needed to be changed, there-by drawing attention to it. In the old world, things always needed to get as bad as they needed to get before individuals were willing to make a change, and he was doing his job well. He was a great motivator and succeeded well in waking up the masses. I think I got slammed with over 600 emails in one hour from folks who were so very angry with me and thought I should be hanged! But this is how it is at the higher levels. Things are always precisely where they need to be, even though it may not appear so at the lower vibrating levels. We are creating as a whole indeed.

- *In the higher realms, we create in alignment with our purpose and geographical home on Earth.*

There is no doubt that alignments are where it's at in the higher realms. Alignments create portals where higher level energy can pour through with ease. The ancients knew this, and guided their lives and ways of being with alignments in regard to the powerful energies of the cosmos and the celestial bodies and their movements. Being in alignment then, in as many ways as we possibly can, will greatly assist us in connecting and staying connected to the higher realms. Alignments create a wonderful feeling of balance, buoyancy, and non-attachment as well.

When we know our soul purpose, or rather who we really are, we can then be consciously in alignment with it as much as possible. When we are creating in alignment with our soul purpose, we can create instantly and effortlessly. Most of the time, it is simply and most certainly a piece of cake to create anything that supports who we are at the highest levels. When we really know what our next step is at our soul level, all the supports will magically arrive for us and all we need do is to jump on board. If you are not yet sure of who you are and why you are here, know that you are not alone. Before we can progress very far in our evolutionary process, we must first know who we are. It is very much our starting point as we evolve spiritually.

Residing in our geographical home on Earth also places us in alignment with some powerful creating abilities. I remember a time when I arrived in Asheville, North Carolina, a beautiful and incredible place. So many people remarked in months to come that they felt like they were home the minute they set foot in the beautiful mountains there. For me, I felt very out of place. I simply did not fit in there. I could not wait to get back to the Southwest. And when I am here, as I am now permanently, I feel absolutely wonderful. The mountains of North Carolina had so many special gifts for me, and the energy there was truly awesome, but the Southwest is the area where I am truly connected to who I am.

Our geographical home on Earth has its own specific purpose as well. And as each high energy spot on the earth vibrates its unique purpose, this purpose is then in alignment with our own individual unique purpose. These dual alignments greatly assist us in opening higher energy portals for us to reside in, there-by assisting in an effortless process of creating anything and everything we need and truly desire. We are then in alignment with our soul purpose at the same time that we are in alignment with our geographical home on Earth.....some powerful alignments indeed!

So once again, when we are connected with who we are through the earth, we create an alignment or portal, and we can then create with even more ease. A section further along in this book called *Identifying Our Geographical Home on Earth* will assist you in identifying your own special geographical space on the planet.

 ## Staying In Alignment With Creating In The Higher Realms

If creating is different in environments of higher vibrating energy, how can we most utilize these new ways on a more regular basis, or in other words, how can we stay in alignment with them?

- We can *stay in alignment with ourselves* as much as possible. This involves not taking things personally, vibrating our true purpose wherever and whenever, knowing who we are, and allowing our desires and creations to support who we are.

- We can *stay in alignment with our geographical home on Earth* as much as possible. We vibrate the same as our homes; we only need to identify what that vibration is…simply, it is what makes us feel the best and makes us come alive with passion and excitement, and a space that we absolutely cannot leave for very long.

- It is easiest to create things that we *daydream* about. Daydreaming places us in a state of letting go or of no attachment. Creations can arrive much more quickly when we simply daydream about them, without a great need for them to manifest.

- We can *be comfortable with where we currently are* by feeling gratitude for this space we are in. We cannot move into a new space with a new creation until we have fully embodied what we have previously created. It can help if we know that what we previously created was right for us then, or in alignment with the "old" us, but we can now create fresh and new as we are always becoming fresh and new ourselves. And in this regard, we can know that we always have everything we need, as we are always right where we need to be at any particular time!

- In relation to the above, *we always create what we are vibrating or what we are being.* No right or wrong, just a law of energy. We know what we are being by what is currently surrounding us. This barometer allows us to tweak what we choose to, or serves to simply indicate what we are about! (In the old 3D reality we usually only notice what feels icky, or in other words, we evolve by means of polarity. Thank goodness this is rapidly changing!) When we are able to accept where we are and lovingly acknowledge it, we are then ready and open for something new to manifest.

- In the higher energies we can create more easily if we create *higher vibrating things.* This is why creating at soul levels becomes more prevalent and why we also begin to create more as a whole as well (as being part of and very conscious of the whole is a higher vibrational way of being and living). In this way, our creations are matching the higher vibrating energies we are now residing in....and this creates another alignment, as alignments are what it is all about in the higher realms. Alignments result in a flow, in smooth sailing, and no struggle.

Focus and clarity are vital to creating during the beginning stages of our evolutionary process, and this brings us to the next section...

 ## Focus and Clarity

The denser the dimension or rather the denser the energies we find ourselves residing in, the more we need clarity and focus when creating. This is because there are so many more energies flying around that have to be waded through and navigated around. It is ever more important then, that we maintain focus and are very clear about what it is that we desire. As we begin to evolve higher, focus and clarity are important as well, but not nearly to the degree that they were in the old reality.

In the higher realms, think of something desirable and it seems to arrive for us in record time, even though we may not have realized that we were indeed creating it. Have we not had the experience of having something we thought we wanted arrive for us almost unexpectedly, and then realize that it was not exactly what we had intended?

"Oops! This isn't exactly what I was thinking of," we might exclaim. But then we get another chance to get it right...oh, the beauty of creating in the higher realms. We can always create fresh and new at any given moment. A special gift of creating anything that does not quite fit, is that it gives us the clarity to create more clearly when we start again with a new creation.

I remember when my friend Nancy, a real estate agent, was showing me parcels of land here in New Mexico. With each new encounter of land, what I liked and did not like became more and more evident, even though I really wasn't too consciously aware of my exact desires before we began; I was just sort of looking around for fun. While being in the space of each new and distinct energy, a picture soon began to reveal itself of what I would be most happy with, but I would not have known this until I had experienced other possibilities. So even though we may believe that we know exactly what we want, at times we really do not know until it arrives for us.

And this is the importance of clarity in the higher realms. The clearer we are, the better our creations match what our purest desires are all about. Another wonderful aspect of clarity is that it gives us the opportunity to know what we really and truly deserve and desire. Clarity in the higher realms is not relegated to what we think is probable or possible...it is relegated to "anything goes," and this is the beauty of a miracle, and miracles abound in the higher realms. (Duly noted here, is the fact that on the beginning rungs of the ascension ladder, the further the stretch with what we believe is possible to what we desire to create, the more difficult the creation.) It can always be great fun to start creating with small and simple things that are a stretch, but that we feel really don't matter if they manifest. The results can be great training for creating what we think may be the impossible.

The more clarity and detail we place within our desires of creation, the more fully they will provide for us what we are seemingly wanting. If we say that we want to be happy, this can manifest with a huge array of possibilities, and also can serve to dilute the energies that are utilized for creation. Becoming clear serves to fine tune and focus the energies where they are needed, and also serves to support and solidify our abilities as very conscious creators. This brings us to the importance of *focus*.

It is no new news that what we focus on we get more of. What fills our minds and consciousness, and how we perceive things to be, is what fills the physical world around us. What we are *being* or vibrating, is what we will be creating as our reality and world.

This phenomenon of focus, then, is also what we can use to navigate in the higher realms. In even higher realities, we can focus on something (a destination), and literally arrive there in physical form. This is the power of focus. This is the power of fine tuning and really learning to utilize energy. Until we are actually in that high of a vibrating reality within and without, one where we can use focus to literally travel, we can still use focus in our current reality to navigate the dimensions, but in a different way, yet even as effective. This is what was discussed at the beginning of the *Keys of Being* section.

When we use focus to create what we want, it is important that we do not spend the majority of our time in this state. This is because we are here in the now, and not in some virtual reality or desire of the future. It is important, as mentioned many times in this book, to be present where we are. We are on this planet to have an experience here, not to try and continually be somewhere else through meditating or the like (the higher we begin to vibrate and evolve, the less we meditate). We cannot create when we are trying to be somewhere other than where we are. Being somewhere other than where we are, places us out of alignment, and therefore out of the higher flow of the energies of alignment.

In the old world, meditating may have placed us in a higher vibrating space of "feeling" or perhaps gaining awareness. And as a health tool for relaxation, what a gift it was indeed. But in the higher realms, it only serves to place us somewhere other than where we are currently residing. We are evolving into states where we are always in a state or energy where mediation was striving to place us temporarily, and thus, we eventually do not need or desire to "meditate." Meditation is a wonderful tool for the old world, but in the higher realms, it simply ceases to exist. As we travel up the rungs of the ascension ladder, we may still choose to meditate, but only for very brief times until we choose it no more.

So then, now that I have probably offended many of you who meditate and perhaps have a different perspective (ouch!), how do we use focus for purposes of creation and being? We can use focus in regard to what we choose to notice or pay attention to. When I go on a hike in my neighborhood, I usually pick up energies there, see portals, and connect to the sky and the non-physical world. Others, who at times hike along with me, find potshards, look at trails and wildflowers, or the like (yes, I do that too sometimes). When my neighbor's dog accompanies me, she sees rabbits. So then, what we are about or what is meaningful to us is usually what will appear for us. What we look for then, is what will manifest.

Are you one who sees the glass half full or half empty? Do you perceive the world as getting better and evolving, or getting worse? Do you believe you are getting beaten up and worn down, or that you are simply losing the older and denser aspects of yourself?

I had a friend once who loved to take care of stray animals, so her focus was on them much of the time. She continued then, to attract stray animals to her home, and they seemed to find her wherever she was. This was what she was about, or where her focus was, so it then became her reality in the physical. I had another friend for a brief time who would not watch commercials on television as he believed they were made to control him. I love many of the commercials because I find them even more entertaining and fun than the television shows!

Focus involves what we are noticing or paying attention to, and certainly our interpretation of what we are noticing. What we do not choose to pay attention to cannot exist in our reality or world. Focus allows anything to exist. So why not apply this law of energy and simply focus only on what we desire to have in our space?

In the beginning stages of residing in the higher realms, focus and clarity are more vitally important than ever before. With so much more of the density now gone, what we choose to focus on now, and how clear we are about what we desire, are extremely instrumental in our navigation and creation process in this now New Reality.

As we begin to evolve even higher, we realize that the trivial details do not matter. Much of everything is incidental and minor in relation to our happiness and peace of mind. We become more and more aware of what really and truly matters the more we shed our old and outdated selves. And this is when the true beauty of love, peace, and joy begin to be ever more present in our lives and within our current reality. We thus begin to focus more on what we are grateful for and on what really and truly matters.

The more we evolve, the more we do not focus on anything, as we are simply *being*. We enjoy the now, as all our needs are met, and are simply grateful and happy right where we are.

 ## Staying In Alignment With Focus And Clarity

- Utilizing focus and clarity as ways of being in the higher realms can be easiest if we do not take them too seriously. Taking clarity seriously, for instance, places us in a state of holding on too tightly, and then we would not be able to benefit from the gifts that clarity offers. If we can focus and use clarity in a fun way, by laughing at and tweaking our imperfect creations after they arrive, and by simply focusing on and noticing the things that bring us passion and joy, we will continue to easily and effortlessly create what it is that we desire.

- We can also use focus in regard to our relationships with others. If we choose to focus on another's special gifts and talents, this then, will be what presents itself to us much more frequently. Have you ever had an experience when you interacted with someone that was completely different than another's experience with that individual? This is because we are somehow focusing on or paying attention to what we know to be true for us, or perhaps what we expect from that person. In this way, our experiences with others can vary greatly from one person's interaction to another's.

- As we begin to evolve into higher and higher states of being, we no longer desire to be anywhere but where we are. In this way, we are extremely contented, have everything we believe we truly need, and are in states of great peace and acceptance. The higher states of reality are all that we truly and easily see, and thus, we need not intentionally focus on anything else but what is right in our spaces and has been all along.

Living Effortlessly With No Struggle or Suffering

In the higher realms, "trying," or having to make any kind of effort, simply does not exist. There are many words in the human language that will cease to exist in a higher realms reality, and "trying" is one of them!

Through our on-going ascension process, we are being groomed into losing much of our old ego energy, or any kind of energy within us that is in charge of making things happen ourselves. The more we find ourselves connected to Source, the more we will find ourselves living in an effortless way. This is because Source, or the universal energy, is doing much of what needs to be done.

Through our on-going process of spiritual expansion, we find that being in states of exhaustion and fatigue has become almost the norm. It seems that getting things done requires more energy reserves than we have in our batteries, or perhaps the burden of having to do things we do not really want to do is draining at best.

There is most certainly a reason why this is so. In higher realms energy, much is fine tuned into its' pristine and purified state. In this way, much else on the periphery that existed in the old world of denser energy no longer belongs. So then, this results in higher ways of being that say that we only do things when the desire arises from inspiration and joy. We only do things that are aligned with who we are and what our passion is about. We only do things, then, that are in direct alignment with the highest vibrating aspects of ourselves. Anything else either belongs to someone else's passion, or is simply on its way to extinction altogether.

Have you ever put off household chores or projects for eons of time, but suddenly had the energy to complete them when you knew that special guests were arriving soon? Have you ever been in a situation where you had to complete something because you committed to it in the past, and now you absolutely have no desire or energy to get going on it or finish it? Do you find that it is increasingly more difficult to do things that you "have to?" Does your energy drop during these times, but quickly rises in other situations that involve things you absolutely love, or even when there is an opportunity to play and have fun with no responsibilities?

Responsibilities play a key role in the ascension process as they most assuredly are on their way out. As we progress through this process, we find that we are no longer able or willing to continue on with many of our old responsibilities. Responsibility energy contains the blueprint of "have to's" and of "shoulds." These energies simply do not live in the higher realms. They cannot. In this way, we may wonder why we can no longer carry out our prior responsibilities and may feel highly irresponsible when we are going through this change!

Staying centered with no stretching or extending is also a manifestation of being in the higher realms. When we are evolving as a whole into this state of being, we find that we seem to be prohibited from leaving our own space. This is because we are learning or being encouraged to accept and utilize this new way of being. Staying put is vitally important. If we exert ourselves, make and effort, reach out of our energetic spaces, extend or push things into happening, we are then no longer in an energetic space where Source can find us. We are thus a moving target, no longer in the space of simplicity, being, or stillness, and what we desire to create cannot then find its target or home base. We are thus out of alignment and there is no portal or vortex present within us. Our channels then become closed.

When we can stay in the center and simply be, then we can live with no struggle or effort. Being in this space allows for the synchronicities to arrive and for others to come into our spaces that are willing and able to provide for us what we cannot provide for ourselves. This is why I do not send the energy alerts to my subscribers within an email. I would be extending and I would not be staying in my own space, which in this case would be my website. The energy would dissipate. When certain energies are aligned and ready to connect, they will! So we need not make everything happen ourselves.

Yes, in the higher realms, at times we find that simply entertaining a thought about something seems to bring that something to us in record time. "Oh my!" you might say. "I didn't realize what I was thinking about until it arrived just now." Or perhaps, "Whoa! Hold on! Too much is arriving all at once!"

Are there situations that exist in the higher realms that feel like effort? Is everything *always* effortless in the higher realms?

In the higher realms, if something does not arrive for us very easily, many times it is because we are on the wrong trail (or rather not in alignment with it), and something much better, which we are much more aligned with, has yet to connect to us. Higher vibrating energy is blocked from interacting with lower vibrating energy. This is the same as a mis-alignment. We are vibrating higher now and thus, as mentioned in earlier sections of this book, we cannot easily create lower vibrating things; there is too much of a stretch.

Another scenario can be present as well. When things are not working for us, it can also be because all our ducks are not yet in a row. When our ducks are not in a row, we create a resistance, if even subconsciously, and block the flow of creation because we cannot say a resounding "yes!" to the entire scenario. Also, if anything begins to feel as though it is too much work and effort to accomplish, that we are pushing too hard, or perhaps becoming impatient, then this is our red flag that something is amiss. We need to step back, wait for all our ducks to be in a row (or rather to be able to say "yes!" to every aspect of our desire), or examine the situation to see if this is what we really want. If we do not know why something is not flowing, we need only trust that we are being protected by our souls, while we ready for something much better to arrive. In this way, it can be challenging at times to create effortlessly when we are evolving so quickly and our desires then change so quickly!

And again, when we want to create something very grand, quite big, and genuinely important to us, then it takes a bit longer to arrive. Bigger creations contain more components, and thus, more ducks to get in a row for a complete alignment that allows for the creation energy of Source to flow directly and purely. The fewer the doubts, the quicker and easier the manifestation.

When we are in alignment and *very sure* about *anything*, it will most certainly arrive for us in a purely effortless way. When we are very sure, we step back. We get out of the way, as we know our new creation is a certainty. In this way, we are able to live a life of effortless creation. Following the path of what simply feels good, with no rational explanation, will always create that space of effortless creation. As mentioned so many times before, when we can arrive in a space of not caring whether we receive what we desire or not, we then create the space of letting go (or non-attachment) and Source can then enter and do the creating for us.

One more scenario needs to be mentioned here as well. I personally believe that this situation is the most common situation that blocks us from creating or seemingly living effortlessly. After we evolve out of the examples given in the previous paragraphs, we now have the ability to create effortlessly as we have certainly evolved into beings that can live in a reality of effortless creation very easily now. So then, we eventually move from creating effortlessly via the ways explained above, into simply creating instantly. Once we get used to this way of instant creation, we begin to expect it, and then we find ourselves in a very new reality indeed. I create instantly the far majority of the time, and know that many of you do as well, so I know this to be a real and true reality for some. But if ever there is a reason we cannot create instantly, I believe it to be this:

There are phases of the ascension process where the energies are simply stopped and we are blocked from creating anything at all, even if *we are* in alignment with what we want to create. These phases occur when we are ready, but enough of the whole has yet to arrive. Thus, we are being asked to "wait" until enough souls are given an opportunity to arrive where we are. This is what creates the continual instances of critical mass evolution and what allows us to move forward into very new territory when the time is right. When a level of critical mass is then met, the energy breaks and resumes its' forward motion. This can be a frustrating aspect of our process, but it is a typical one. If we allow ourselves to be the loving and patient beings that we know we are, have come to a point where we are happy and contented no matter where we are, then we can happily wait for others to catch up. It is much more difficult to create individually during these times because we are going against the tide and thus blocked, but in the end, we always end up right where we need to be. At the highest soul levels, we are creating and participating in this amazing Shift of the Ages, and thus, know exactly what we are doing, gladly agree to participate, and are very much connected as a very supportive whole.

So then, when it is the evolutionary plan that is blocking our manifestations or our move forward, there will always eventually be a huge break-through when it is time. It is then that we resume forward movement and arrive in our very new spaces with our very new creations. And we get to have our brothers and sisters alongside us as well!

As we evolve higher and higher, we create as a whole much more frequently indeed. It is then that we begin to experience what we have known all along...that each and everything in existence eventually affects and is needed by the whole...and that we are indeed, all one.

"This is too much to absorb at once and all too confusing," you may be thinking. "I will never remember all of this and I am simply too tired to want to! There are too many scenarios. Can't you make it simple, Karen?" To sum things up:

- At times when the higher energies are ever-present, we create so quickly that we are given an opportunity to tweak our creations into exactly what we desire, as they can arrive in a form that we may decide is not exactly what we had in mind.

- At times we can be stopped from receiving what it is we think we want because we are no longer in alignment with it. I.e., we are now vibrating much higher and are then ready to receive something much better, only we had not imagined something as grand ourselves. Higher and lower vibrating energies are not in alignment.

- At times we can be stopped from receiving because all our ducks are not yet in a row. In other words, we do not yet have all the pieces required to create a particular thing. Some things that are required for this creation are still on the way to us, or perhaps we cannot yet say "yes!" to all aspects of what we want (we are not yet in alignment).

- When we find we are pushing or desiring too much and nothing is manifesting, 1. We are not yet ready or, 2. We are being protected from an undesirable outcome. When we are truly ready, we are truly aligned, and are not then surprised when we receive what we are in alignment with. At a deep level, we simply "know" that it is time. And we usually "know" when we are very relaxed in regard to our desires, as there is now a good fit. We can still passionately desire, of course, but when we desire in a much more detached and relaxed way, it can really make a difference. If we know it is time for our desires to manifest, and they still do not, then we are being protected from a situation that will harm us. Remember, Source knows more than we do at times!

- At times we can be stopped from receiving when we are waiting for more of the whole to catch up. In other words, the energies are waning because more souls are still adjusting and aligning, and when enough are ready, the energies always resume in a wonderfully big tidal wave. This is the way of the highest level of creation...creating as a whole.

During times when we are feeling blocked from creating what it is we think we want or need, all we need do is relax, forget about it for awhile, focus on what we have now and what we dearly appreciate, and take a break. This places us in a space of no struggling or suffering, and we will find that when we are in this space, we are truly in Heaven indeed.

There are many times during the ascension process where many of us gave up our desires to relocate or move our residence...there were just too many roadblocks and too much effort and struggling was required. We seemed to have the knowingness that what we need now do was to appreciate where we were and make our current home the best it could be. We were so wise indeed! But then eventually, a new critical mass was reached and our old desires and dreams very suddenly began to manifest. The doors flew open and we had to re-adjust once again. Phew! What a wild ride this process can be!

We can easily disregard the complicated explanations above and use this simple key to live effortlessly:

Enjoy where you are, focus on all that is beautiful and all that already exists in your present reality, be oh so grateful for it, be present with it, disregard the rest (or do not give much attention to it), and you will find yourself in a reality of effortless creation and continual gratitude. In other words, be in the now.

One day, I was feeling out of sorts for no particular reason. Things just did not seem right and I was not my usual happy self. I was wondering if perhaps a change was in order. That day, I had a phone conversation with my father. He asked me how things were going. I proceeded to describe to him that I had the most beautiful piece of property anyone could ever imagine. I told him how I loved my work, how it fit me to a tee, and that it was effortless. I told him that my health was very good. I told him how truly beautiful it was here in New Mexico with the flowers blooming and the beautiful clouds and red rocks. And as I described my life, I realized that I was living the life of my dreams. So what in the world could I possibly be unhappy about? It was then that I reminded myself how grateful I was for what I had created and where I was in my life. If someone were to have described my life as their's, I would have immediately said, "I want that life!" But I already had it.

We always have everything we need right now. Our Heaven then, is HERE right now. It is not out there somewhere where we are not. We can easily overlook our own Heaven by spending too much time in the reality of what we feel is not working.

So what about struggling? Why does struggling cease to exist in the higher realms? We struggle because this is all we have known in this particular incarnation. ..*up until now*. We are very used to struggling and programmed for struggling. When things arrive easily and effortlessly, we may find ourselves quite amazed and most certainly thrilled and surprised. All we seem to have known up until now is that we have to go around the block to get across the street. Nothing seemed to be direct in the old 3D reality. In the higher realms, energy is always very direct, and simply goes in and then out. This is why our new children are so direct. They are already programmed and ready for the higher realms, and simply do not understand why we go around and around, and explain and rationalize so much.

In addition, the ascension process creates a state within us where we are simply too tired to make anything happen. We can do no more ourselves. In this way, we are forced into connecting to Source, as we cannot make things happen from our own ego minds (the ego minds that are slowly leaving!). Through the ascension process, the struggle then ends. And this is precisely when Source comes barreling through the door and takes over for us.

Struggling is not a part of higher realms living. I began writing this paragraph just after I came in the house from pulling some weeds in my flowerbeds. The day before, I had done some weed-eating around the house, and thought that I would wait until we had another of our beautiful August monsoon rains before I attempted to pull the weeds in the flower beds. I thought that the ground would be softer then, and make things much easier. It had rained the night before and the ground was perfect. As I began pulling the weeds, some of them would not budge. "Well," I thought to myself, "I am simply not willing to make a huge effort and to struggle through this project. If I have to struggle, I simply will not do it and will just let it go." Suddenly, as if by magic, I looked around and the project had been completed...with no struggling.

When we come to a place where we are absolutely no longer willing to struggle, then we will not. We have known struggling for so very long that it has almost become a way of being for many of us on this planet. I finally decided that I did not care if I had to leave this world, but I would never struggle again. I had had enough. And this is when we begin to find that struggling ceases to be a part of our reality. After I had completely let go of my brief marriage because it was a continual struggle, I almost immediately felt a very new presence around me.....a presence of someone very new. It felt truly heavenly and brought me to tears. It felt like a great gift from above. I had known that this person was always a possibility if ever I were to find myself alone again, but had thought it best to give my marriage as much as I could first. "Where has this person been all this time?" I asked the universe. The answer I received was this: "You first had to let go of thinking relationships were about struggle." I thought I had done this long ago, but as always, there are frequently leftover tendrils!

Because we are so much more connected to Source in the higher realms, we no longer need a struggling experience to serve as a connector or as a vehicle to encourage us to let go, and thus connect to Source. Struggling also derives from resistance. Giving up and surrendering to Source and our higher selves or souls immediately places us in the energy and reality of the higher realms. We can relax, breathe deeply, and enjoy where we are. The continual wearing away created by the ascension process places us in a space of exhaustion and letting go as well, which is another great by-product of our spiritual evolutionary process.

And what about suffering? Suffering existed in the old 3D reality as it served to connect us to Source as well. When we suffered, we surrendered, let go, gave up, and realized that something needed to change....and usually it was us.

Suffering made us go deep. We were forced to go to the depths of our souls and to examine and question much. If we had lives that were always perfectly blissful, we would never be encouraged to question, grow, expand, and ask for something different. But now that the new reality is upon us, most of us are ready for a world of no suffering.

Why? Because we had to suffer in order to get into a state where we became very clear about what it was that we really wanted. We had to suffer in order to arrive in a place where what we wanted and desired was devoid of our ego selves. We had to be ready and primed to create things from a higher place, before we could then begin creating the New World. We had to suffer to realize what was really and truly important to us. Most of us believed that suffering was the only way to make a change. It seemed to be the only thing that got our attention.

Suffering got all of the old "crap" and peripheral desires out of the way. It fine tuned us into who we really were and made clear what was really important. And in this way, we were then newly poised to begin this very new journey into the New World and to begin creating from a higher vibrating stance of purity in our intentions and purposes.

In the higher realms, we do not need to suffer to connect to Source. We remember our suffering experiences through the ascension process we experienced from prior years, and no longer need to go there. We have learned much, are vibrating higher, have released a great amount of lower vibrating energy within us, and suffering is then no longer needed. We are much more connected now, and certainly much wiser beings.

We can now more easily create from the pure intent, knowingness, and the pure original purpose of our souls.

Staying In Alignment With Living Effortlessly

How do we continue to live a life of effortless creation? How do we get across the street without having to go around the block? How do we let Source do most of our creating, while we simply stay in our joy, bliss, and purpose?

Very simply.....**let go.** This is all that is really needed. Or, we can follow some of the keys listed below:

- Following our hearts, connecting to what makes us feel good and come alive, allows us to stay on our true and rightful path. In this way, we are creating from the higher vibrating aspects of ourselves...or our souls (and not our ego minds or what remains of our dis-connected selves). Staying in the space of our passion as much as possible, keeps us focused mostly on that, and Source can then do its' job in creating all our peripheral supports, as that is not our job to do.

- We can wear our "one hat" as much as possible, and know that this "one hat" is what we came to do and be. Our one hat is all that is ours to do. It is the purest expression of who we are. All else is up to others, to Source, or will simply no longer exist in our reality of the higher realms (pretty much the same as following our hearts).

- Relaxing, and knowing that we are totally being supported by Source and our souls can help as well. *Know this, as it is an unquestionable and unwavering truth.* We are here to facilitate the ascension process. We came together as a group of souls to accomplish this task before we can then move on to the next higher vibrating reality. We are very advanced beings (if you are reading this, you are most certainly one). We are being lovingly watched over by the remainder of our soul families in the non-physical, as they are so very excited at what we are accomplishing. We have most certainly reached the critical mass stage in many areas. Thus, there can be no error now. We were not meant to suffer and to be left behind. We are at the helm. We are being supported in every way. Our needs will always be met. They are supposed to be. Any fears, lack of support, danger, or abandonment can now only arrive from an illusion within our individual thinking, or perhaps an individual victim consciousness. All that was meant to be ours in order to facilitate the creation of the New World *will absolutely be ours.*

And so it is. Absolutely and most assuredly....and so it is.

- If receiving all we need is not effortless, it was not meant to be or our ducks are not yet all in a row. Stepping back, waiting a bit for things to shift and align, or changing course can then greatly help.

- We can remember that we came together as one big amazing soul team to create this Shift of the Ages. Thus, at times, when we are waiting for a critical mass to be reached, we can remember that we are creating and moving forward as a whole. In this way, we can be reminded that we are just in a waiting period, know that things will move forward effortlessly when it is time, and simply enjoy where we currently are.

Shutting The Door Behind Us

One day I received an email from a woman who used to teach me yoga. This beautiful and special woman was currently in the Hawaiin Islands, where she had been for a month or two after leaving the mountains of Flagstaff, Arizona for an indefinite stay in the islands. She had been called to the islands for reasons that had yet to become clear to her, and she was confused. After we had exchanged a few e-mails, she received her clarity (of which she already knew, of course, and was only getting validated), and then returned to Arizona. When she arrived back home to the mainland, she e-mailed and asked when I would be back in Flagstaff, as she wanted to connect. It just so happened that I was going to be there in the next few days. Although not close friends, it seemed that this meeting was an important one none-the-less.

As we connected over a cup of tea, she suddenly gave me a very important message. This message hit me so powerfully, and validated so intensely what I had been seeing for some time now, that I had no doubt that this was the purpose of our meeting.

She told me that she had been concerned she might not like the islands or fit in there. Her friend who was currently living there immediately corrected her by saying, "No. It is really a matter of the islands *liking you*." He then proceeded to tell her that she or anyone for that matter, is not automatically accepted by the locals. If the locals do not feel comfortable with someone, they will not accept them or open up to them, which many times encourages that person to leave. For those they love and accept, they will embrace and welcome with open arms. Her experience in the islands proved to be more than she had ever hoped for. She said that she had never felt more love, caring, unity, and support at any other time in her life, and greatly missed this energy when she returned to Arizona.

The Hopi tribe here in the Southwest has a similar philosophy. They will not allow just anyone into their world. I have found them to be some of the most welcoming, loving, and open people I have ever known. But if you cross them in an inappropriate way, they will not hesitate to take appropriate legal action against you. They know their boundaries.

After spending much time at the ancient sites here, I believe that a very similar philosophy was present with the ancients as well. The ancients utilized what I refer to as "cover sites," or sites that presented a passive, peaceful exterior of feminine energy which was only what they allowed to be revealed to a visitor. One particular site, perfectly poised at a bottleneck entrance to the Mogollon community of many other scattered sites, was utilized for much trading and was thus, very open to the outside energies. This particular site was poised in an area where visitors and travellers would most likely end up as they first neared the Mogollon community.

Not openly visible to its many visitors was the fact that it was really a "cover site" which encouraged outsiders to believe that what was revealed was all there was. And hence, not much interest was promoted for continuing on past this site and into the Mogollon community. Other powerful and valuable energy and ways of being were hidden beyond this site, but one might never know as these ancients revealed themselves to most as very simplistic and plain.

Many other individual sites were macrocosmically laid out in this fashion as well. Behind a "cover," or area of each site which would be accessed first by a visitor, existed some very powerful acitivites and structures that were simply being protected from any intruders. A simple more basic existence was revealed first...usually a farming area or area for community trading. But if one were allowed to traverse further into each site, one would encounter the real purpose and power of the site.

So in this way, not everyone was allowed in. As the Mogollons were a peaceful and highly evolved culture which still contained the pristine energies of the "very beginning," these sites were being protected by the powerful but subtle energies of illusion. In addition, the ancients vacated their communities in one big whoosh many times. This was because they were very aware at a higher level that lower vibrating energies would be arriving in due time. They knew then, that they must indeed leave, as their higher vibrating cultures would then be contaminated and dominated by this newly arriving energy belonging to other individuals. The ancients left when they knew that the tide had turned...that the tide had turned and another lower vibrating reality was ineed on its' way. In our current reality now, it is just the opposite. A newly arriving *higher* vibrating reality is on its' way.

In many areas on the planet, this same scenario is happening now. Whether it be higher vibrating countries being invaded by much lower vibrating countries, cities and towns being over-run by different cultures that are bringing in some lower energy, or simply a dominance of dis-respectful, new, and unaware employees taking over a workplace. This is occuring because we are indeed switching over, but the higher vibrating energies are still in the minority. In this way, those bearing more light are retreating to their sanctuaries, relocating to new and different geographical areas, or simply buying land and staying put until the fall is complete. Eventually, the majority will be comprised of higher vibrating energy. The see-saw effect of transition can be tricky at times, but as always, everything is transpiring in a divine and perfectly orchestrated way.

The law of spiritual hierarchies supports this reality as well, because higher vibrating energy cannot exist alongside lower vibrating energy. If you were to look through the dimensions, you would see a perfectly orchestrated and divine plan at work. There is no judgment with this plan, as it is simply a matter of physics and energy.

So then, it is part of the evolutionary plan to "shut the door behind us" after we arrive in a higher dimension. We are not required to allow everyone into our spaces. It is perfectly OK to have healthy boundaries, and with the higher dimensions breaking down many of the old denser energies, our boundaries are more fragile and thin than ever before. In this way, it is vitally important to stay behind "the veil," or rather, within our higher vibrating creations and spaces. We have lost many of our old defense patterns as they were vibrating lower. In this way, it can now be difficult to exist with less boundaries, and with the now more innocent and pristine energy within us, when our outside surroundings are vibrating so much lower. We may feel very vulnerable and defenseless in a world that still seems to present a threat.

This situation of shutting the door behind us is perhaps one of the most important of any of the aspects of the ascension process if we are to remain sane, and may even seem strange since unity is such an important concept in a higher vibrating reality. The higher we begin to vibrate, or the more evolved we become, the more uncomfortable it is to be in any aspect of the old world or old reality. Spending any amount of time there can serve to throw us off balance, make us feel extremely uncomfortable and edgy, make us wonder if we are indeed residing in hell, and break us down into a weakened state.

If lower vibrating energies cannot be in the same space as higher vibrating energies, why do we need to set strong boundaries at all?

Boundary issues become ever important the higher we vibrate. This is because energetic boundaries are now much thinner. There is less density present, just like in the very higher realms where the angels hang out, for instance. But at the same time, because we are going through an ascension process, things are a bit different. In the reality where the angels hang out, there are no threatening, dangerous, or lower vibrataing and lost energies! We may be residing with less density surrounding us, but most of us are still embodying some traits that vibrate lower. So then, because we are continually in transition through this process, we are getting a little of this and a little of that as we move up the rungs of the ascension ladder. In so may ways, this transition creates one big mish mosh, as we are not yet completely here or completely there.

In this way, we may still find lower vibrating energies within our spaces. Why? Because there is an overlap somewhere, or rather a matching energy beween ourselves and the "unpleasant" intruder, and we have then created an open door. The matching energy might simply be an instance of two individuals wanting to develop new friendships, so they might both have that in common. Or perhaps two individuals both enjoy bowling. When the two individuals are focusing on and connection soley through bowling energy, things may seem to feel pretty good, but then one individual begins to demonstrate lower vibrating behaviors and the relationship then becomes uncomfortable for the one vibrating higher.

Any overlap energy creates an open door. Thus, there then exist energies in our spaces that are not a match at all, as they have arrived along with the overlap energy.

Another scenario involving boundaries relates to those who are seeking light, but want to get it from another person. In this way, an individual who is bearing more light will feel drained, used, perhaps abused, maybe even violated, and eventually wants to flee. One individual will be very happy and the other individual will be very uncomfortable. The more light we embody, the more we will attract others. This sets up a situation requiring an understanding of healthy and necessary boundaries.

Navigating the Dimensions...Staying Sane and Connected While in the Lower Vibrating Energies

There is a solution to this dilemma and/or aspect of the ascension process involving boundaries, that can keep us in the higher realms and allow us to remain balanced, in states of peace and joy, and living our dream lives while wondering if we have indeed arrived in Heaven.

Of the many ways of being that we eventually evolve into, there are three that become important and extremely helpful in regard to navigating the dimensions and staying sane.

1. *Letting go of compassion and moving into love.*
2. *Letting go of supporting and allowing others to suffer.*
3. *Protecting ourselves while in the lower dimensions through the energy of love.*

These states of being might sound cold and incaring, but I can assure you that anything else only derived from a 3D way of thinking and being. So many times I have said that the higher realms is not what we may have imagined it to be, and this is yet another example. As we begin to vibrate higher and expand and grow, we indeed find that what we might have believed to be a higher way of being, quite simply, was not.

During my lifetime, if I had heard it once I had heard it a million times... "You are such a compassionate and caring person!" Little did I know how much this trait would eventually bite me as I evolved. It first began when I found out that my neighbor, whom I dearly loved, was recovering from a kidney stone. I cared so deeply and resonated so deeply that I got a kidney stone within a week. Several weeks later my sister-in-law and both brothers were having trouble with nerve pain in their legs along with lower back pain. The next day, I had the same, but this time, only briefly. Next, my step-mother was scheduled for surgery to remove a lump in her thigh...hopefully not cancerous. Within a day or two I developed a lump on my thigh. Jeez! What was going on here?

I soon discovered that deep caring and compassion vibrated lower than love and only existed in the old reality. Each time that I cared too much, my energy would literally drop down lower and I would connect in an unhealthy and non-productive way. Over and over I had this experience. One particular evening I was concerned about my prior husband from a brief marriage, as we had recently parted and I was very worried about him. Suddenly, in dropped my non-physical companion (who only shows up rarely with *very important* messages ☺), who very susinctly told me that I was running my energy completely wrong. Oh, how he loves to catch me when I am going down the wrong road and hurting myself!

Well, after weeks of getting this message, I nearly had a breakdown as my identity was severely compromised. After sadness, tears, grave disappointment, feelings of being invalidated and seemingly worthless, I finally began to get the hang of shifting out of my old self and into someone new. I simply did not know how to shut off my feelings of compassion and deep caring. If I could not be the me I had been my entire life, who in the world was I now supposed to be? Was I supposed to stop caring about others? Was the main component of the way I ran my energy now being completely shut off? And I have to say, I now felt completely shut off myself....turned off, shut down, and eliminated! But eventually, I found a new way, became a new me, and was on my way once again.

As always, the ascension process continues to make new people out of us. This is why we may often wonder who in the world is staring back at us when we look in the mirror, and may wonder just who is speaking the words we hear coming out of our mouths. We eventually lose an awareness of ourselves as we embody more and more Source energy within us. And this is how it is.

So then, when we are in states of compassion and deep caring, we are giving energy to and fueling the situation which we are compassionate about. Resonating too much with a situation which is not ours eventually becomes ours if we resonate too deeply. We end up going where we need no longer go. We need not make another's journey our own. We are no longer vibrating at that level, so then, situations or experiences which require compassion are not longer in our own individual realities. In this way, being in states of compassion takes us to the old world and the old states of being that will drag us down. Love is the key here. We can still show our deep caring and concern, but we can now show it in the form of love.

Love vibrates very differently and much higher. Love tells another that "I respect your journey, as it is yours." Love tells another "I know that what you are going through is part of your soul's desire and plan." Love tells another that "I love you always and know you can handle your situation." Love tells another that "you are deeply respected and highly revered." Love tells another that "I am here to listen." Love tells another that "you matter to me." Love tells another "I will be by your side."

So what about the energy of support? Are we supposed to quit supporting too? Do we get to have any positive and helpful traits at all? As a life-long supporter of the dreams of others and the many situations of others, this one was a tough one for me as well.

In June of 2008 we experienced a substantial movement of energy with the arrival of the solstice on June 21st. It seemed that nearly everything was knocked out of its groove and left flying around with seemingly no familiar home. We had reached a very important turning point in the ascension process and this event created a very new state of being for many of us.

It was now time for "the fall" to begin in earnest. Many with the gift of sight and vision had predicted that 2008 would be the year of new beginnings and great abundance for many. But by June, nothing much had changed and many felt down right awful at best. Where was all that abundance? Where was our very new beginning? We had decided as a group of souls to give as many as possible the opportunity to expand, awaken, change, and grow...to make perhaps different choices in their lives....choices made without regard to money or perhaps with a new knowingness of what was really and truly important to each and every one of us. This then, created the big delay in this new time of very new beginnings.

So then, the solstice of June 21st added to this very important phase. Much was shaken up, much was usurped, and insecurities, suffering, confusion, and choas resulted. It was a very difficult time. But not only was it a difficult time for those who were suffering, but it was difficult as well for the loved ones of the suffering, even if they were very fine in their own lives and circumstances.

At higher levels, those who had gone before and were thus more situated, were being prompted to stay out of the fall, to stay out of the suffering, and to simply stay put where they were. This manifested in strange ways, but basically, many of us had to watch from the sidelines. Why? Because our presence alone in areas that were falling would only serve to hold them up longer, and they needed to go. Many of our loved ones still needed to hit rock bottom before they were willing to wake up and make a change. Thus, saving them or supporting them by holding them up and possibly aleviating their circumstances would only serve to hinder the very needed fall. Individual souls needed to come to a point where they were ready to "ask" for help, or for something new and different. They needed to be ready and willing to *let go*. Holding them up through our supportive energy would only serve to prolong the existence of what needed to fall. Thus, supporting was seemingly prohibited.

During this time, enough had now crossed over to "the other side." When this occurred, everything else was most ready to fall. It was time. The other side was secure and safe....a place where all our needs would be met in an effortless way. And going down with the fall was not our original intent or plan. Most of us bearing light have been very used to supporting or bringing light into situations, and now this role was over forever. Done, never to return. We had accomplished a monumental task and now we could rest. No more supporting, holding up, extending, and infusing our energies into the old and denser reality to hopefully bring it "up."

Who were we now? What now was our very new role? Without being able to be compassionate and supportive, what in the world were we supposed to be doing with ourselves? Could we no longer simply brighten anyone's day, or were we now supposed to shut down and become invisible?

Very simply, we had successfully crossed over to the other side. Here, there is no suffering. Here, compassion is then no longer needed. Here, we need not support or hold anything up as each and every one of us can hold their very own space with the support of Source energies and our own bright lights. Here, we can easily and effortlessly create whatever we choose, all by ourselves. Here, there are no ties that bind us. Here, we need not hold the energy for another, ever again.

But what happens then, when we need to leave "here" and visit that old world in another reality that is still partially poised in the lower dimensions? How do we assist others who are still traveling up the ascension ladder or who are being seriously affected by the fall? And when we need to interact with some of the old systems, as we still sometimes do, how do we do this without suffering greatly from all that old and very unpleasant energy that nearly kills us to be around?

Love is our greatest protection. Over the years I have heard of different psychic remedies providing so-called "protection" from dark forces or the like. But the higher we evolve, the more we realize that keeping our own vibration high is the best protection ever. Intentionally doing anything is not a way of being in the higher realms. *Sending* light to others, smudging to remove denser energies, or even surrounding ourselves with light eventually becomes very moot. There is too much extending here and too much of our old ego selves making things happen. In the beginning stages we may have felt more comfortable performing these rituals, but eventually we will find that we no longer need them.

Staying in a state of love as much as possible when we visit the denser energies or old reality is all we need do to stay centered, peaceful, and grounded. But at times, this can be a very tall order indeed. After all, we are only human and still evolving. This is why we can only stay in these denser energies for limited amounts of time and then we must retreat to our sacred spaces. It may sound harsh, self-serving and a bit strange, but it is a good and solid remedy to keep us afloat and feeling good so that we *can* assist others in our own special ways. As always, a simple fact of how energy works is that higher vibrating energies cannot stay in the same space as lower vibrating energies.

Just like a simple flower in nature, when we know who we are, are very comfortable being just that, can stand firm and steady within our true selves, not taking things personally, and simply being comfortable with our true, authentic, and divine selves, we can then be much less affected by any lower vibrating energies which may surround us.

Add to this, being in a state of love as much as possible and feeling this love for our brothers and sisters while seeing who they truly are...their true, authentic, and divine selves, can greatly ease our time spent in the lower dimensional realities.

When we find that we are suddenly in the company of an energy which does not feel good to us, it can help if we stop to identify what our overlap or like energies are about.....in other words, why we connected in the first place. Staying in that arena or subject matter as much as possible while ignoring any others, along with focusing on the divine gifts and talents of that individual will greatly assist in keeping our lights shining and our vibrations high when we are not in our sacred spaces.

We are most certainly morphing into the angels of the earth, one by one. As our angel wings continue to sprout (that never ending stiffness and pain in our upper back and neck ☺), we become more like the angels who have loved and watched over us each and every day. So then, eventually we will *be* the angels of the earth, as we drop down into the lower dimensions to assist and serve, while spending the remainder of our time in our Heaven on Earth.

By simply *being* who we truly are...our pure and authentic selves...we can thus keep our light shining brightly while we make our own special contributions through our sacred gifts and talents.

Do you know who you really and truly are? Do you know what your very special contribution is? Do you know why you are here on this Earth at this particular point in time?

~ Stepping Stones on Our Path: the Masculine ~

In the year 2001, I suddenly began a series of intense challenges which involved panic attacks, continual insomnia, wild and horrific dreams which occurred whether I was sleeping or awake, and what felt like some kind of horrific breakdown. These experiences, among many strange others at that time, became acutely unmanageable by me, so I sought medical care as I knew I needed help from somewhere. Little did I know at the time, that I was smack in the middle of the beginning of my ascension process.

I found myself truly blessed to have a loving, caring, and talented team of healers along with me for the beginning stages of my journey. One of these healers was a conventional counselor named Sherri. Charging a meager $10 for each session, as I was unable to work during this time, she was an angel in every sense if the word.

Never once did we review my life or go back into my past of horrors and abuse. Sherri instead used her talents to draw out my own special gifts and talents, helping to guide me on my path of creativity, allowing me to find my true and authentic self, and thus, my panic attacks eventually subsided. And because of this special experience, I knew from that point on that I would *always* know who I was, and that this new awareness could never be taken from me.

Knowing Who We Are

As we progress through this unusual and very challenging ascension process, so much of who we thought we were is purged and released. What is left is the pure gold nugget of our true and authentic selves. Each and every one of us has a multitude of special gifts and talents, and a light that shines ever so brightly. We are all unique, like no other, and what we have to offer and the way we offer it is as different and unique as each and every snowflake on a beautiful snowy day.

Before we begin creating a very New World, or a world that we may have always known within our hearts and in our highest visions, we need to first know who we are and what we are here to contribute toward making that world a reality. Please know as well, that there are some souls currently residing on the planet that are simply here to observe and are thus just here for the ride. None-the-less, for each and every one of us, it can greatly help to know who we are, what our strengths and weakness are, and what makes us tick. Our strengths serve to highlight our contributions and our service to humanity. And where we are lacking, are areas that another will fill with their own strengths, gifts, and talents. In this way, all is always in divine and perfect order. We no longer need to wear all the hats as we need only know what is ours to do.

If there are things we do not particularly like doing, or have no interest in, it is because there is another soul who absolutely loves doing those things. And if *no one* likes doing those things, they will then cease to exist in a higher vibrating reality. There would be no energy to keep them alive and in existence. What we focus on and hold in our consciousness is all that can exist in a higher vibrating world.

So then, who are you and why are you here at this particular time? The majority of us are not consciously aware of who we are. We seem to know that there is something that we are here to do, but we cannot quite grasp what that something is. At times this feeling can cause a sense of disconnection, frustration, feeling lost, or perhaps an intense longing to connect with our souls.

"I'm *me*," you might say. Or perhaps, "How do I know? I don't have a clue!" Ask anyone who knows you well, and they will most likely be able to tell you very easily who you are and what you are about. We can never really see ourselves because we are within ourselves. Ask anyone on the outside, and he or she can see you much more clearly. This is how psychics do readings. A psychic, intuitive, or sensitive person has a gift of being able to "see" from the outside, and to see very clearly what we cannot see from our subjective standpoint. Psychics are able to rise above much of everything and to see from a distance. But our friends who know us can see us very well indeed, even if they are not particularly psychic!

The ascension process is very rooted in clearing away the debris. This massive clearing process results in the loss of density, or the loss of much that is no longer needed. In this way, there is not much left that stems from a subjective standpoint, or from our old dense filters of seeing things, as there is much less "din" or mis-perception energy now present. Anything that is left then vibrates higher, is purer, and we are thus automatically catapulted or placed in a very new residency of a higher vibrating reality. This now higher vibrating self is what gains us access to the doors of a higher dimension that we now match within us. When we reach this new reality, or higher vibration, we can then see things much clearer indeed.

We eventually come to see that there is no black or white, right or wrong, or much in between as our "opinions" are just that...old filters. With these filters, opinions, or ways we viewed things much more out of the way, we are then left with a specific purpose unique to each and every one of us. We are also left with a desire to leave the old mainstream of entanglements, energy games, or our many old connections far behind. We now know who we are, why we are here, and are very ready to get on with that purpose.

When we are able to focus from who we are the majority of the time, know who that is, and are able to stay in alignment with our "mission," we can then more easily remove ourselves from what is left of the entanglements that the denser energies create. Identifying who we are is thus an important first step in this process, as we can jump off from there at any given time. Our purpose vibrates very high, never changes, and can always serve as a foundation, connecting point, or if anything, will keep us in alignment with the higher realms and with our original soul intention. This one area of knowingness is a vital component in creating a stronger connection to Source and to our souls. And staying in alignment with who we really and truly are, creates an opening or natural portal to the higher energies of Source, thus creating much more joy, miracles, ease, and flow within our lives.

How can we know and remember who we are? When we have been ourselves for so long, in a subjective sense, how then do we know who that is?

You might start by asking those you know and trust some simple questions:

1. What am I good at?
2. What am I continually interested in?
3. What do I talk about the most?
4. What am I the most passionate about?
5. What would be a good career or job for me?
6. What do I complain about the most? Why? (Creating the opposite of that can be a part of our purpose as well.)

7. What do I do so easily, that I am not even aware that I do it all the time, when   most others cannot?

8. If there was an event or day planned around a specific subject, what would it have to be about that would allow me to drop everything and attend?

9. What personality traits do I possess that are obvious to others, and that you noticed the minute you met me?

10. If you were to encounter me as a mass of energy and vibrating colors, not knowing who I am, how would I *feel* to you? In other words, what energy do I posses and how is it readily identifiable? Am I gentle and loving, passionate and confidant, or perhaps strong and caring? Am I still and centered, or do I flutter around here and there? Am I light, heavy, or grounded? In other words, what is my essence or how do I come off to you?

Then ask *yourself* some of these questions (you will most likely want some paper and a pen or pencil to jot down your answers):

1. Due to unusual circumstances, you suddenly find yourself dropped on an isolated island with no

apparent inhabitants. You must set up some kind of living arrangements. What do you find yourself attracted to the most in regard to making life comfortable there? What would you strongly desire that someone else do, if there was someone else there with you? Why would you do what you chose? What is it about this choice that is so very important to you? Then once again ask yourself why your last answer is important. Continue to ask yourself why until you arrive at an answer that is a very simple statement. Is this something that you find yourself providing to others in your current life?

2. You have relocated to a small community recently, and there are no stores, businesses, or much of anything for at least 200 miles. Shortly after your arrival, the world sustains several immense natural disasters, and communication and supports from the outside world are blocked from your community for at least a year. The several hundred members of your small community get together and decide to delegate various roles and duties to all the inhabitants there. They desperately need everyone's help, *and know at some higher level that*

you have a *gift, talent, or great interest and knowledge about something they could use* to help set up a sustainable community. There are enough residents with enough talents present, so that each and every one of you has the luxury of providing whatever he/she chooses. You feel that this is a great opportunity for you as well, as you will be able to provide your services with no interference what-so-ever from outside sources. You also know your service or talent will be needed, acknowledged, and appreciated, there will be no hoops to jump through, and you have wanted to provide this service somehow for a very long time. The other members of your community are so happy that you offer what you do, because there is no one else that can provide this service. What is it that you offer your community? Know that they willingly accept what you have to offer, trust you immensely, and are greatly appreciative of your services. Anything goes; what is it that you get to do for your community?

3. In your current life here on Earth, what were your favorite subjects in elementary school, in junior high

school, and up through your highest educational level? What was it about each of these subjects that you enjoyed? Do you see yourself having any interest in these areas today, and throughout most of your life? What was your favorite part of your favorite job, or if you rarely had jobs, what was your favorite part of a favorite project you were involved in? Why? What was it about this thing you were involved with that made you come alive and kept your interest so intently? Why would these areas of interest be important to a world or community? What would your interest areas offer the inhabitants of a new world that would lift them up and bring them joy?

4. A dear friend of yours is suffering, as she/he has just experienced a loss. Your friend has been moping around for awhile now, and cannot seem to get back on track. What do you offer her/him? What is so very easy and natural for you to give? What could you give that would brighten this person's spirits and make them feel better?

5. Whom do you admire the most in this world, whether present or past? Why? What is it in them that you so

honor and respect? Know that these traits are greatly within you as well. Now list several more individuals that you admire, ask yourself why, and know that you possess these traits as well. These traits are the essence that you possess...the way you appear to others...and how you naturally express yourself.

6. If you watch television, what shows do you continually find yourself watching? Why do you like these shows? What do any of them have in common? What books do you continually find yourself reading? What do they have in common? What section of a bookstore do you find yourself naturally gravitating to or what kind of stores do you frequent the most? What subject matters keep coming up in regard to the questions in #6? What is it about these subjects or themes that are important to you? Why? How do these subjects or themes relate to your passion or interest area? In other words, what can you bring to these areas that are so very *you?*

7. On five small pieces of blank paper, write down five things that you feel you *must* have in your life, or life

would have no meaning for you. Now take one of these things and discard it, leaving four behind that you absolutely *must* have in your life. Continue on until there is only one piece of paper remaining. What, then, is the most important thing to you? What really and truly matters in your life? What is it about this one remaining item that has the most significance to you? How does this one remaining item play a part in what brings you joy? *In what way do you interact with it (or what do you bring to this one remaining item)? Why* then, is it important to you?

8. Looking back on your entire life, what were your happiest moments? What were you doing, who was with you (or perhaps you were alone), and what, if anything, did any of these moments have in common? Was there simplicity in any of them? What were these moments about?

9. Take a deep breath, find somewhere comfortable to relax, and clear your mind as best you can. Ask your non-physical star family members to join you now and to support your memories so that they may easily arrive for you, piece by piece. Even if you are not

consciously aware of your star family's presence, simply trust that they are there. After taking several deep cleansing breaths, close your eyes, place your feet flat on the floor, and then open your eyes and begin reading: Once upon a time, you had a home in a world where everything was just about perfect. There was no suffering, pain, distress, so called darkness, or disconnection from Source. Each and every morning you would wake up to an incredibly beautiful day, with love ever present, peace abounding, and a feeling of being safe and contented that was always a certainty. Surrounding you were loving and supportive friends and beings, all divinely connected to a whole, with one special purpose. You felt totally and completely fulfilled. This was a place, or perhaps a star, where you were really you, where you resonated beautifully and perfectly, and where you fit in, in absolutely every way. This place was *you*, as were all its other inhabitants. It looked like you, felt like you, smelled like you, and had very specific colors that felt oh so like home. This "you" has been around for eons of time, and is extremely engrained within your soul. (Breathe deeply again and relax your mind and

body....close your eyes and see if you can *remember.*
If you cannot remember, that is OK too.) This real
you runs incredibly deep. Know as well, that you
were always "seen" here, as each and every being
there honored and revered who you were and was
very aware of what you were about. Your star or
home vibrated with a singular purpose, besides the
shared purpose of a connection to Source and the
whole of the universe. You and all the other
inhabitants united together daily, doing things
related to and focusing on one particular thing that
you all had in common, even though each of you
contributed in very different and unique ways. What
then, is this one particular thing or purpose that
exists so deep within your heart? Each and every
one of you was very devoted to and very good at this
one particular purpose. You were all experts at it
and were frequently asked to contribute your
expertise to other areas of the universe, when there
was a need for your very special energy. And in this
way, you were invited to attend and to create the
Shift of the Ages on planet Earth at this time,
bringing with you your very special purpose. What
are you here to do? (For example, my continual role

has been to lay foundations, to get things ready, to prepare and set up, and create the needed structures and formats, to get things ready and functioning, and then I leave, not staying within the creations. This role has been paramount in many of my 3D jobs, in my relationships with others, and within my life as well, even though at different levels.)

10. What do you know the most about? What are you considered an expert at, or when do others continually seek your advice and revere your expertise? What is your piece of the New World to set up? What is *expected* of you, as you are such a natural at it? What are you dedicated to expressing and providing? What is it that never leaves you, even when you have experimented with many other different interests? What do you hold within you, that you feel you absolutely *must* get out into the world? And in what modality will you offer it? A creation of art, a writing, a form of music, a nature modality, or perhaps something very unique and different?

After you are finished writing down your answers to the questions above, look through your notes and see what common themes or messages are woven throughout. See if you can pull them altogether and come up with a shortened theme or purpose, and how you express this purpose or passion. What road will you place your gift or contribution upon?... Which brings us to the next stepping stone of our journey:

Defining Our Path

After we have defined what it is that we wish to express or contribute, it can greatly help to define where we will place this gift, or the road or path we will place it upon. Say, perhaps, that you are here to bring information about the earth to the planet. You may have had an interest in earth related things your entire life...and perhaps one specific thing relating to the earth really lights you up. Where then, would you express this passion and how would you bring it to the world? Would you be a tour guide or perhaps a writer? Would you make videos of your passion? Would you create incredible paintings that depict the beauty of the earth and connect everyone who sees them to your vision and purpose? Would you sing songs or make music about the earth? Would you create a sanctuary for visitors? Would you give talks or lectures about your area of expertise?

Are you a communicator through public speaking? Do you like to entertain? Do you prefer to remain behind the scenes and write books? Are you perhaps a guide who loves to give tours or even to guide others by way of individual sessions or videos? Are you more comfortable at home or out in public? Do you like to travel, or would you prefer others to come to you? Do you need another to fulfill the purpose of getting your work or expression out there, or are you one who loves to get the work of others out there?

In other words, what is the most comfortable vehicle for your purpose or gift? What particular vehicle fits you just as well as your special purpose fits you? Most of us are utilizing our vehicles now, have for a very long time, but might not be consciously aware of it.

Writing works best for me because I am extremely sensitive and like to remain behind the scenes. If I look back into my past when I was younger, I did not realize it at the time, but I loved writing in elementary school. I always seemed to be involved in some kind of news or newsletter project in my later years, and remember that journalism was a fun and exciting subject for me. Being in the limelight and out in public only serves to shut me down, and thus, I am not nearly as able to bring forth my passion and energy in this way. My sensitivities are just too extreme.

Others thrive while out in public, and being in the limelight, being in front of groups and out with people really lights them up and makes them come alive. This then, is a good arena for them. We are all very unique and different and will quite naturally gravitate to our own individual arenas.

But if we can come together with our brothers and sisters...if we can fill each niche with our own individual gifts and talents, and thus, create one big whole....then we can also be united as one while we bring forth our own special gifts and talents.

Connecting With Our Soul Teams and New Communities

When we arrived here on Earth for this particular incarnation, it was decided that the best of the best would be here. In times past, there were ancient and advanced souls who incarnated, and their presence greatly served to enhance the planet. These beings stood out like no others. For them (and many times they were really "us"), these experiences were their passions, or simply a way of enjoying themselves and experiencing form. There was no specific purpose of raising the vibration of the planet, even though this was usually an outcome none-the-less. It was simply an experience of "experiencing" form within another creation of form (or a planet); all just games of creation.

This time, there are *many* of us ancient and advanced souls here all at one time. In actuality, most *all* advanced or highly evolved souls are here now, including many who have *never* had an incarnation on the earth, and some are simply here to observe the process and the plan in action while in form. Other souls who have never been here in form before are here because their representation was needed and required. These special souls frequently feel very challenged here, as the planet Earth is much too harsh for them and they feel completely out of their element. These unusual souls are being very lovingly watched over and protected by their families from "home," even while these families are biting their nails waiting for the ascension plan to complete! But representation was needed by every existing creation in the universe, so as to embrace and capture all of life in order to start again. Others are the fore-runners or leaders of the plan, and in this way, have done much, been about everywhere with their soul histories, and feel very guided to participate in this last and very paramount expression of energy within form. In other words, there are representations from every area of the universe for this miraculous Shift of the Ages.

Infusing our energy into form was intended to be one big, fun game. Energy can infuse into form in ways that are more exciting than our limited 3D minds could ever have imagined. One common occurrence was when many of us infused our energy into one form. For instance, several of us may have inhabited the form of Jesus or of Mahatma Gandhi, all at one time. In this way, several of us were able to experience this drama or play all at one time from the same perspective.

Being that the ascension process creates a melting down or a spinning off of all our infusions into form since the very beginning of our creation from Source, we then become the purer gold nuggets of our original creation. This is why we feel so connected to each other at times, as we have been together for eons of time and have played together with energy for eons of time. We were also created around the same time as well, and thus our energies are vibrating in much the same ways, as energies that arrive (or are created) at the same time arrive on the same energy "rays."

This process of ascension then, brings us ultimately to a connection with what I refer to as our soul teams, or in other words with the souls we intended to connect to through specific divisions of purpose.

There is a divine plan here for those frequently referred to as "lightworkers," and part of it involves a pre-plan of coming together for our shared purpose relating to the Shift of the Ages as well as the creation of the New Planet Earth. At the given time, we will thus be united with those souls who have an overlap or shared energy and purpose relating to facilitating the Shift of the Ages, as well as coming together for the creation of the New Earth. This uniting process is divinely orchestrated, and overrides the Law of Attraction, as most anything relating to soul energy always overrides everything else, as it runs the deepest and vibrates the highest. In this way, we will be united at the appropriate time with members of our soul teams.

In regard to people in our lives, there exist instances when the original divine plan cannot be orchestrated, or when there are changes made due to different choices of each soul. It is a loose plan in some regard as there are so many of us. So then, there is room for various connections to change as need be. For instance, we may have planned on uniting with a soul at a particular time, and one of the souls is not yet at a point where a union can take place. Or perhaps we have made new and different choices in our lives, and this then, creates new and different scenarios. When these kinds of things occur, we are always given a "back-up" or new soul to unite with. There are so many of us waiting in the wings, or rather a large pool of advanced souls for us to mingle with, that our souls can easily re-arrange their plans and thus still be able to continue on with their journeys....journeys which individually reflect what stage of the ascension process each of us is now on.

We progress at different times...although generally speaking we are usually fairly on track, and in this regard, there are always enough of us to keep each other company. If one union does not work out for various reasons, then there is always another soul close by that will fit us as well. So then, there is never, and has never been *one* particular soul mate for us, as there are *many*. And each experience of unity brings a new and different outcome with a new and different experience!

Another prevalent scenario is when two souls part, as they each have a new and different role to now fulfill. I had a union and deep friendship with a wonderful man for 10 years, and then suddenly we parted. We had been together since the beginning of time, were deeply connected, and felt very much a part of each other. I was told and could see as well, that he had a new and different purpose to fulfill now, as did I, and we were no longer on the same "team." The energies on the planet had shifted; the masses had reached a new plateau, and thus, new doors were now opening. When the energies and vibrations on the planet reach a certain frequency, our programming kicks in and we are then activated into a readiness for our next mission or purpose.

Very shortly there-after, a new man was introduced to me (my brief marriage), and this man was much more in alignment with my next "assignment," or with my new purpose at my next level. Although this man and I were brought together for a specific reason, we eventually came to know that we were simply at two very different levels and needed to part. Some souls are comfortable moving forward, expanding, letting go and taking the opportunities given to them, and others are not willing and ready to open and move forward. Even though opportunities may arise for all of us, it is always a choice by each soul whether to take an opportunity, or to stay in their original spaces and patterns. When this occurs, we are then given more choices and are then matched up with souls who are a much better fit for each of us.

We are always matched up with others who most closely match where we are currently vibrating, or at higher levels, matched up with where we currently are on our soul paths in regard to what we are here to offer. If you are one who vibrates a lot of *soul energy*, for instance, you will usually attract others who are a match in regard to the higher vibration of soul energy. In this way, we might become confused as to why we are connecting with those who do not seem to share or interact with what is left of our "issues," or mis-perceptions about how to run our energy. Or, we may attract to us an individual who has not yet progressed as far as we have in regard to behaviors (or "issues") and conscious awareness, but who none-the-less is an ancient soul as we are and shares our vibration of what we have to offer the planet at this time.

In this way, it is our soul energy which is creating the union. It is our souls who are uniting in similar purpose; so it is not necessarily a union then, for the purpose of clearing old energies or evolving our personal vibrations. The more we evolve, the less we unite with others for the purpose of clearing, purging, and balancing our own individual energies. Ultimately, and this is happening now, we will unite for the pure purpose of enjoying each other's company and creating together. And that is when it can feel heavenly indeed! Pure companionship, fun, and bliss, with no purpose, plan, or work to bring to the planet is then our reality.

So what about our soul teams? When do we connect with them and how in the world do we find them? And when do we finally get to reside in the new communities?

At times it can be challenging to be alone and wonder when oh when will we ever connect with our soul teams, with what seems to be our brothers and sisters, and with our true families of origin that feel oh so comfortable to us. We were seemingly dropped here on a seemingly spiritually desolate planet, all alone, far away from home, and into a reality that may have felt upside down, inside out, and perhaps even frightening.

As the density begins to dissipate, or what has filled in the gaps in regard to disconnect energy, mis-perceptions, and much else which did not vibrate very high, we are then left with more "room" to navigate and to "see." The ascension process ever so slowly removes that density, and the more this occurs, the more readily we will be able to connect with our soul teams. When there is not much "in between" (in regard to the "in between" being the lower vibrations), we are then able to connect "through" and "to" the higher vibrations which are left. And this is when our soul teams begin to loom ever closer.

"Opinions" vibrate lower. They vibrate lower because they represent energy that is still being interpreted through a filter. The higher we vibrate, the less we see through filters, as we come to see from the core energies of love, understanding, unity, trust, respect and value, and the like. Strong opinions with an "I am right and you are wrong" attitude only serve to create division. The truth of the matter is that nearly most of the time (but not always) *everyone* is right and we need only combine all these beliefs. The ultimate higher vibrating scenario, which will eventually occur, is one in which we can all see that we are going in the same direction, only we each have a very pivotal piece of the pie and only need to integrate these pieces together. Each piece will eventually carry a high vibration when each piece is ultimately refined to its highest state.

In the very small town where I currently live in New Mexico, we have no library. But we do have an awesome bookmobile that comes to the post office once a month. I absolutely love this bookmobile! Stepping into this bus filled with books and incredible librarians is like heaven for me. I always feel as though I am in some other world when I am there. Not only do the librarians give extraordinary treatment and service to us patrons, but the books lining the shelves are the cream of the crop. I have never seen so many high quality, superb, the best of the best, and the most awesome variety of books in one place. It is as if anything mediocre has been weeded out and only the higher vibrating books are there. Although small, the variety is incredible along with the quality. It is truly a wonderful and divine "small."

One day I became tired of all the clothes in my closet. Although I liked all of them for various reasons, there seemed to be too many. I decided then that I would only keep the clothes that were truly awesome and which I felt wonderful and very comfortable in when I wore them. Anything else I gave to charity. In this way, I truly felt like I was the best me and felt wonderful whenever I wore an item of clothing that really looked good on me. If anything was so-so, I got rid of it. My grandmother was known as being a very smart dresser all her life. Although she did not possess a large wardrobe, what she had was of high quality and timeless. And in this way, she developed quite a reputation as a woman who was always impeccably and divinely dressed.

So then, as we weed out the denser energies within and without, we will eventually unite with the cream of the crop, or in other words, the highest versions of our soul teams and brothers and sisters. When we have a distinct purpose or passion, and know (whether consciously or not) that we are here to contribute this to the planet, nothing can seem to hold us back.

But know as well, that things can go awry when we get too caught up with our own purpose. When this occurs, we seemingly have no room for the purpose of another. It can seem then, to be our way or the highway. There are many roads to heaven, and when we are open to combining each and every contribution to create one big whole, then we are truly on our way to creating a heaven on Earth.

Our own very special contributions were meant to be utilized, revered, and requested. It is then that we are "on." The remainder of the time was meant to be spent in the company of our brothers and sisters, having fun and enjoying ourselves. A problem arises when we forget, run too much of our energy all the time, and become someone who is "on" with our purpose and gift all the time. Now that we are residing in higher energies, we are thus infused with more energy than ever before...and this can create too much of a good thing. The higher vibrating energies can activate our purpose and magnify it to a degree that it now becomes a liability.

This is why we may forget to honor the contributions of others and may believe that our way is the only way. We may think that our gift is what everything is all about, as we "see" everything through the eyes of our gift. This is when we cannot seem to see outside of ourselves. And this is when we forget that we need to have fun and enjoy ourselves when we are not being called upon to use our gift or contribution. I can assure you, that our individual ways or contributions are only ONE piece of the pie that is needed and necessary. We can give ourselves a break from our purpose, enjoy life, and simply enjoy each other when our piece is not needed at a particular time.

As I write these words in August of 2008, we are in the midst of a presidential election here in the US. Two candidates have risen to the forefront, and each candidate represents a specific political party. Each of these candidates vibrates with an energy of the "center." One candidate was born bi-racial, thus containing an energy of a unity of black and white, is known for embracing the whole and listening to all sides, and the other candidate does not represent the standard of conservatism which is normal for his party, as he is somewhere in between and much more of a maverick. These two candidates represent where we currently are on the planet as a whole...*we are balancing our energies and finding a center.* These are manifestations of the awesome progress we have made indeed, as it is now very evident in form.

This is also an example of how extreme energies are now becoming defunct. So then, as we begin to come together as a whole and to vibrate higher, extreme energies begin to balance themselves out, becoming less aggressive, losing their "I am the only one!" vibrations, and it is then that they begin to vibrate higher. In this way, unity can then be much more successful, as when energies are balanced and more finely tuned, they can then be utilized in more appropriate ways...and not in extreme and divisive ways. (It would be the best scenario possible if the highest vibrations of our Republican party here in the US combined with the highest vibrations of the Democratic party, to create a higher vibrating whole. But we are simply not there yet as a critical mass, even though we have made progress in recent years.)

When we come to finally realize that each and every contribution is vitally important, and when we come to contribute in ways that are balanced and not so extreme, then we are left with a wonderful whole. We cannot wear all the hats. We need our brothers and sisters to contribute what we were not intended to contribute, and what we are too tired to contribute ourselves! We need to allow them to do their parts, and to trust and know that in time, they will do their parts well. We will all do our parts well when we have refined our parts into a balanced and healthy state, and when we are willing and ready to allow others to do the same.

This is what has held up our unity process for so long. ..we were not yet at this point. As we come to balance out our energies and to refine our own special gifts and talents, we are doing this for the entire universe as well, as we represent all of creation. We have a very special and vitally important role to fulfill, and I believe we are doing it well. We are the forerunners and the way-showers. We may carry an enormous amount of responsibility, but it was intended that we stumble and fall, that we learn and expand as we go, and that we are always doing the best we can. We are all in this together, and even though it may not be apparent at times, we are supporting and helping each other during each and every step along the way.

When we become angry or resistive to another's contribution, as this other contribution seems to conflict with our own, it can greatly help to remember that their contribution is not ours...it is theirs. We need only focus on what is ours to do. When we can appreciate and accept each other's contributions, therefore enjoying them instead of feeling that they are different and we cannot relate, and they are perhaps hindering ours, then it can truly make a difference. When we are willing to let go of wearing all the hats, usually through exhaustion or letting go of our ego selves, we can then enjoy the benefits of unity and the whole. Each and every one of us is striving to create a higher vibrating whole, and we are programmed to do it in completely different ways. There is not just one road to heaven. When we combine all our roads, we will then have a massive highway to support us and arrive in heaven with ease!

The long delay in connecting with our soul teams is also due to the fact that the planet needs to be vibrating at a certain level, and we need to be vibrating at a certain level within ourselves before we can connect firmly to our soul teams. The time has to be right. And the time also has to be right in regard to creating the New World. All these things are connected. We may have embodied special and very intact visions within ourselves of what the New World would look like, but until enough of the planet is *willing* and *ready* for a very New World, a New World cannot be embraced or even allowed to happen. We need to be ready as well. For most of the year 2007 and 2008, it was all about reaching a balance point within ourselves, as we adjusted our energy in massive ways. This process of balancing will continue on for all of us at different times, as we are all at different levels of our process.

So now, our soul teams are certainly more ripened to come together. The time is better, there is less density present, and we are also much more in alignment and ready as a planet to begin creating something new. In addition, there are much more of us poised and ready now than ever before, and this alone will serve to tip the scales.

All said and done, how do we connect with our soul teams, or in others words with those who will share our particular contribution to serving the planet and for creating the New World?

Soul teams and communities will not necessarily be one and the same for each of us. So then, our soul teams will comprise one group and our communities may comprise another. Our residential communities vibrate higher and may come later than our soul teams and here is why:

Our soul teams were designed to assist us in connecting with those souls who are instrumental in uniting with us in regard to our service to the world, or in relation to bringing our service-oriented gift to all of the planet. In this regard, our soul teams exist in a reality that vibrates lower, as it is connected to the entire whole, and not just to our higher vibrating communities of physical residency. Our soul teams exist on the dimensional line, or at times within the lower vibrating dimensions, and our communities exist in the higher vibrating realities or dimensions.

A brief blueprint looks as follows:

We will eventually be residing in small communities of similar purpose. Until we are residing there 24/7, or in every way with every aspect of our being and without the need for money, we will also be connected to our store-fronts, or our methods and portals for receiving money. In this way, we receive money while we are assisting all of the planet in eventually arriving in these communities. So then, the soul team format may vibrate a bit lower as it needs to exist in a lower vibrating reality. Lower and higher vibrating energies cannot exist in the same space for very long. Higher vibrations become grumpy, depressed, lost, stressed, and panicked and lower vibrations cannot see the higher ones, as they are near invisible to them. There are other details to be mentioned here, and they will be discussed in the section *Setting Up Our Store-Fronts* further on in this book.

Our soul teams, then, will be comprised of souls with passions and areas of expertise that fit into our individual plan for service; thus creating a mutual overlap in the needed areas that will then create a whole. In other words, our soul teams come together to comprise a small whole, or a whole which is about our service to humanity. And at times, soul team members can come and go as their vibrations seem to change at any given moment! I cannot tell you how many web designers I have lost because they began transitioning and expanding.

For instance, currently the key players of my soul team are my publisher, whom I click with very easily and who is just perfect for my needs, and my brother, who is very talented at computer programming, web design, and internet operations. These members of my team have to have one foot in one reality and another foot in another reality. My brother is very savvy about the ways of energy and spiritual matters and my publisher is building a house off grid for her large family and stays away from traditional publishing and the mainstream as well. They both have a higher vision and *are* that vision of their individual professions, are still able to contribute their purposes while staying out of the mainstream to a degree, and thus, are very instrumental in bringing forth the energies of the new reality.

Soul teams do best together when each member is very good at what they do, and certainly when each member has a lot of integrity. It is then that they are ready. They are in alignment with their passion and with themselves, and they usually continue to tweak their purpose continually, in order to keep it at a higher vibration. They are thus, very successful at what they do. These components make for a good soul team that can stay together for a long while.

So then, how do we connect with our soul teams?

Firstly, we must be ready by embodying as much as possible what was mentioned in the previous paragraph. Then.... as with most of everything in a higher vibrating reality, we need only stay still, in our passions, and simply *be*, in order to connect with our soul teams. We need not look for them or try and seek them out, as this would only serve to place us "not at home," or in moving energy, and then we would not be there when our soul teams were ready to connect. As we become more and more involved in our passions and purposes, we will naturally attract to us others who share the same. My publisher was referred to me long ago by a man I barely knew. And my brother simply volunteered his services as he wanted to see my web site done pure and clean, and in the highest way possible. He was adamant about this purity, and so very devoted! Now I could not get rid of him if I tried.

I can't tell you how many times I have had a correspondence from someone who has told me that they just *knew* we were supposed to be doing something together, and I am sure many of you have experienced the same. This kind of interaction is forced, and therefore, not necessarily one of a higher order, even though the parties involved may feel very strongly that there is a divine connection at hand. It comes more from the mind than from the soul. Souls will naturally find themselves in similar company through synchronicities, as this is how it is in a higher realms reality. These connections come when we are out of the way and our soul guidance is more at the helm. No planning, no agendas, and no appointments or set timetables. So although we can seem to feel these forced connections somehow, it does not necessarily mean that a further connection was meant to be.

In addition, the higher we begin vibrating, the more our connections will be local. *Local* will become more and more predominant for various reasons. We are refining our energies though spin-offs and through the continual releasing involved with the ascension process, and this leaves much less intact. Our vibrations are then much purer, and in this regard, we eventually begin attracting less to ourselves from farther away places that are not vibrating where we are. The higher we vibrate, the more we condense and the more we bring back home into our own arena. I live in New Mexico, my publisher lives in Maine, and my brother lives in California, so we are certainly scattered! But the best of the best for me in this particular arena has not yet arrived for me locally. Things begin to get much simpler then, when more and more of the "in between" has fallen away.

So what about communities? How are they different from soul teams and when will we connect with them?

Soul teams are designed to assist humanity. As the fall begins to rapidly progress, those residing in what is falling are going to need help. The further they fall, and the more unpleasant their lives become, the more willing they will be to ask for help and thus, the more they will be ready and willing to receive it. In order to assist in the best possible ways, a team is certainly the best way to go. We cannot wear all the hats ourselves...we did much of that in the old 3D reality as it was not yet time for our powerful and light-filled soul teams to manifest. The soul teams (or store-fronts) will thus exist on the dimensional borders. Our spiritual communities will exist far in another dimension and be safe, secure, and completely removed from the lower vibrating reality that is falling. Our communities will be growing and thriving, and the old reality will be falling. In this way, we were not meant to hold up the old or to keep it going.

Eventually, we will find ourselves gravitating to new geographical areas that now match who we are at our highest levels, or rather our true authentic selves. As more and more of us reach these higher vibrating stages, we will find ourselves in similar geographical areas of similar purpose that match our own individual purpose. The higher vibrating areas within and without which have been left intact, will now attract us very naturally indeed because like energies attract like energies, as well as through our soul's messages and guidance.

When we begin to feel it is time to relocate, or perhaps we are feeling restless and *quite done* with where we are currently residing, it may be our soul prompting us to finally find our geographical home on Earth, and this ties in with finding our communities as well.

Identifying Our Geographical Home on Earth

Here is an easy key that can assist in identifying our geographical home on Earth: If we feel as if we no longer desire to move on, or to be somewhere else, we are most likely home. If we feel very situated, contented, and at peace, we are most likely home. If we dearly miss our current geographical area of residency when we are traveling for a while or not there, it is most likely our home. When all of our eggs seem to finally be in one basket, or all in the same geographical space, we are most likely home. Most importantly, if we have no desire to leave where we are, then we are most likely home.

As mentioned in previous sections of this book, our geographical home on Earth has its own specific purpose as well. As each high energy spot on the earth vibrates its unique purpose, this purpose then, is also in alignment with our own individual unique purpose. These dual alignments greatly assist us in opening higher energy portals for us to reside in, there-by assisting in an effortless process of creating anything and everything we need and truly desire.

In years past, many of us were drawn to certain geographical areas for the purpose of shifting the energies there, as well as for the purpose of shifting and balancing the energies within ourselves...as always, all in the same. This continual moving around by those bearing much light was a highly driven urge, and at times, we may not have consciously known why. This process greatly assisted in supporting our grand Shift of the Ages, or our ascension process as a whole, as we represent the whole. Anyone who holds a substantial amount of light makes an impact wherever she or he is, simply by her/his presence alone. But now that we have made so much progress within ourselves and as a whole, we are then able to finally find a permanent geographical residence on the planet that greatly matches who we are; or in other words, a place where we can be truly blissful and at peace forever more. We are then, getting closer to our Heaven on Earth.

When we are living in our geographical home on Earth, we feel right. And feeling right also allows us to open and relax, therefore allowing Source energy a door to enter through us. So again, when we are in our geographical home on Earth, we are a match to who we are; and this state of being, then, supports our creative abilities even more. Our geographical home on Earth then, is always in alignment with our soul purpose and who we are. We are then able to create at the highest levels, what we came to create and what we are about. We are thus in alignment in many ways and this then, places us in our true and rightful power. It is truly awesome when it all comes together.

As we are progressing very rapidly now into a way of being where there is no suffering, pain, density, darkness, and only joy, love, ease, and blissful companionship, our geographical homes will now reflect just that. We will be situated and drawn to areas where we can truly be who we are at our core levels, where we can create all we have ever wanted to, and where life is one big effortless experience of joy and serenity....a joy and serenity which matches who we are and what we are about in every way. It is then that we will have encountered one big piece of Heaven, and it is then that we will be able to create much more effortlessly than ever before what it is that we have come to create.

So how do we initially find and identify our special and unique geographical homes on Earth?

The way is the same for much of everything we create, or in other words, for much of everything that we align with in as many ways possible (the same thing as creating...we attract what we *are*). So then, we *do* nothing. No looking, searching, or intense desiring on our part. When it is time, and we are ready and aligned, our perfect places on the earth will simply *come to us*; their presence will be made known to us through messages, synchronicities, and repeated themes. And we will have a strong desire to be there, as these places simply feel like home.

In the late summer of 2007, I knew I was "done" where I was residing in the mountains of Northeastern Arizona. I felt suddenly dis-connected from my area, but was tired of moving and had no desire to ever move again. I loved the many portals where I lived and felt very at home with these wonderful openings to the sky, along with the energies of the many ancient ruins that surrounded me.

Although I loved my geographical area, I was at the same time craving a sense of community, as there was not much of one there. I had tried to become involved with and to support the community there in many ways, but had been rejected at every turn. So very suddenly on a clear fall day, I decided to get away for a short two day road trip. I needed a change and thought a short trip would do me good.

At that time I was married to Phil, and thus we went on this trip together. As we got into our vehicle and began to drive, going nowhere in particular, we eventually stopped for some lunch at a roadside café in a very small town about an hour and a half away in New Mexico. The café was run by its owners...a wonderful couple from Switzerland who had come for a brief stay and ended up staying permanently. We noticed aromatherapy oils for sale on the shelves, and it seemed that everyone knew most of everyone else.

As we looked out the window, there was a farmer's market going on, with an enormous group of eclectic individuals involved. Lots of home-grown produce, baked goods, and crafts were being sold. There were long ponytails and braids on many men and women, as well as cowboy hats and boots, sandals and tie died shirts.

"What kind of place is this?" we wondered. With not a store or business around, it was a very small community indeed, but a very involved one none-the-less. We remembered it well, as it was so different from our own area, but did not give it much thought after that, as we were in this area just for a rest and change of scene. We were not looking to move anywhere.

During our get-away, we embarked upon a hike at El Morro National Monument, a spectacular spot that had been visited by the archaics, the Zunis, the early Spanish settlers, and now many present day sightseers. In olden times, all who passed through had left their marks and messages carved upon the massive stone walls that comprised much of the terrain, and there was even an enormous ancient ruin at the very top.

As we found ourselves walking the magnificent trail at the top of the volcanic structures there, we encountered a ranger who was overseeing things, making sure that everyone was safe and accounted for. Very strangely, he began speaking to us like he had known us forever, and as though we were actually a part of this spectacular place...as comrades or colleagues, not as visitors. It was then that he mentioned that he lived in the community of Ramah, and absolutely loved it there.

During this time, it seemed that every time I was still or out in a vast expanse of nature, my non-physical star companion would appear and greatly urge me to leave the area where we were currently living. This was unusual, as he rarely appeared unless it was something extremely urgent. "You must leave these lands," he would say. "But I don't want to move!" I would holler back.

About two weeks later, Phil was giving a tour at the ancient ruins where we lived in Arizona. There were only two participants on this particular tour. As the tour progressed, it became clear to Phil that this couple was quite unique, as they were artists and tuned in very easily to the energies at the site. They were from Ramah, 110 miles away across a vast expanse of wide open land, in a completely different energy pocket. They had even built their home in the center of some ancient ruins, and chosen their land when an invisible hand had rested upon the shoulder of one of them during their first encounter with the land.

Near the end of the tour, the gentleman of the pair grabbed Phil by the shoulders, seemingly out of the blue and said, "You *must* move to Ramah. You would love it there and fit right in. Call me and I will show you around." Well, here it was. The unmistakable signs were present. We knew we had to move, and that we had found our place of community at last.

As the days progressed, I decided we ought to go out to Ramah for a visit. In a town of only 400 inhabitants, it seemed best to rent a house in order to have a place to stay while we were getting to know the area. We felt the chances of finding a rental were remote indeed, but this was none-the-less our desire. We had not come up with any kind of a plan yet, when one day I jumped in the car on a whim and drove the hour and fifty minutes to Ramah. I turned into the town and drove right into a wonderful little house with a "For Rent/For Sale" sign at the front. By a series of miracles, it was rented to us for several months, the only rental around, and we were set.

And this is how it is when the time is right. The doors seem to fly open and we easily and effortlessly fly through. So we need not "look" for our geographical homes on Earth, as when the time is right, they will call to us, come to us, and invite us there all on their own.

In a higher realms reality, waiting for an invitation is of extreme importance. In the 3D reality, more than naught we decided what we wanted, we frequently made it happen, and we exerted our will upon our desires as we at times barreled through situations in a forceful way. But the energies were not vibrating as high at that time, and this was the only way we knew how to get anything accomplished. These old ways are not tolerated well in a higher vibrating world. Being one who was used to "making things happen," this adjustment has been an interesting one for me, but becoming oh so very weary of doing it all has been a great help in shifting into this new way of being.

When we are still and can accept and be contented with where we currently are, our new endeavors will *find us* all on their own...and it might not even feel as though it was our idea at all!

How do we then, connect with and find our residential communities? And are they the same as our geographical homes on Earth?

It should be mentioned here, that as a planet, we are still very much in transition. A New World will not be fully ready to manifest until 2012. In this way, some of us may not end up in our final communities or geographical homes on Earth until that time. For me, New Mexico is an evacuation point. Although I am fairly comfortable here, Arizona is my final resting place. The energies of New Mexico do not match my energies nearly as closely as the energies of Arizona do. So in a sense, I am a refugee so to speak for a few years, or until it is time to return to Arizona. 2012 will not manifest as a dramatic end, as it will simply mark an end which has arrived after much has already fallen...but more importantly mark a very new beginning.

"Well, just confuse me even more," you might be thinking. "Is there any way you could just explain things in a simple, direct way, without all the crazy scenarios?" How about this: We are always right where we need to be. We do not need to know what is going on and why. If we feel a strong urge, desire, and need to relocate, we need only follow our hearts.

Whatever area feels good to us is good enough. There is no right or wrong. If an area feels good, then we will most likely begin to get more messages, synchronicities, and signs. Feeling good where we are is all that matters.

Being in transition enables us to be right where we need to be at any particular time. For many of us, we may not be living in our perfect place until after 2012. And for some, arriving there early may be what has transpired. By following the path of what feels good at the time, we are always right where we need to be.

Right before I decided to start drilling a well on my land here in New Mexico, I suddenly had a thought that perhaps there was a better spot of land out there somewhere and maybe I just did not know it. After all, was I *really* sure I was in the right space? I had never felt completely right about my land in all ways. I had never gotten a "sign" about this land, although the purchase of it went through in 24 hours, as well as it being on the market for just one day. So I sat down and consulted some non-physical ancients in the area. I knew I would be connecting with and communicating with beings from the stars on a regular basis, and wanted to make sure that this land was going to work. Well, they proceeded to remind me of what I had come to know many times before, but in my stressful state, was seemingly forgetting (I frequently freak out when I have to make a big commitment and cannot see a thing). They said that it did not matter where I lived. They said that I need only pick a spot in the area, and then *make it work*. They said that it was entirely up to *me*. There was no right or wrong. What was important was that I decide, be sure about it, and then make it work. You see, hesitancy is what blocks creation. At times we may think that someone or "something" knows more than we do.

So then, if you are one who feels a desire to relocate and do not know *where* to relocate, I would first suggest that you wait for a place to *invite you*. If there is an area that feels truly awesome to you, you might want to just go there and make it work. If it is truly right for you, you *will* get an invitation in some form. At times we may not recognize an invitation when it arrives, but any mention of or communication from your area unrequested by you, is most certainly an invitation. If there is an area that you have always loved and been drawn to, but you seem to be blocked from going there at every turn, then I would say that it simply is not time. Follow your heart, make it work, but at the same time, go with the flow that is being revealed to you.

If a geographical spot seems right to you in every way, you absolutely love it there, you feel more like you there than anywhere else, then you are probably in your geographical home on Earth. Our perfect homes match us in as many ways possible. Again, you may be one who is the first to arrive in your permanent spot on Earth. It may feel like Heaven there for you, but no one else has arrived yet. Or, you may be like me and be in a temporary home, but be making the best of it none-the-less as it fits you in many ways, but not in *all* ways. Whatever the case, where we are is usually in alignment with where we need to be at that time. For me, my community in New Mexico is perfect for what is occurring for me right now and for what is occurring on the planet as well. I needed to be far removed from the mainstream. So in this way, we are *always* in alignment with where we currently are....or on the way to getting there!

So then, we will be residing in communities during the fall and after the fall. We will be residing in communities that will be removed from what is falling, whether they are temporary or permanent communities for us. And we will be residing alongside of souls who are with us because they are in alignment with our vibration, our soul plans, with where we currently are now, and as soul companions for pure enjoyment and fun. And yes, you perfect community can be in a metropolitan area as well.

Very basically, communities are comprised of residential areas of mutual interest and of what each soul vibrates or is about. Unlike our soul teams for service to humanity, we relax more with our community soul teams... we interact with our community soul teams when we "are done." They provide a space where we can simply enjoy each other's company and play while we easily and lovingly provide each piece of the community pie through our own special gifts, talents, and areas of interest. There is no helping, saving, holding up, healing, or uncomfortable energies here. All our needs are always met, we live in an effortless and easy way, and joyful fun is abounding. I know this to be true because I have this now. And if I can have this, anyone can.

Living Without the Need for Money

Our current system was designed with money as the means of acquiring most of everything. In this way, much focus has been placed on money. If we need money in order to survive, or to have our needs met, then how would we ever survive when our sources of money run dry? What do we do when the economy goes sour? Or when we lose our jobs? Or when our businesses dry up? Or when, or when, or when.....?

During this monumental Shift of the Ages, we are transitioning from a monetary based society to one that is not. So in this regard, our interactions with money may seem to wax and wane as we transition. One common experience many of us have with the ascension process is when we suddenly lose our jobs and cannot seem to find employment anywhere. What is occurring here, is that we are now vibrating higher than the old system, and are thus ousted from it. Or perhaps we find that we just cannot be in that old space where we once were for one minute longer. And thus, we have a very strong desire to quit our current jobs, but may find it hard to rationalize quitting when we would have no source of monetary income at our disposal. As always, what is within us is vibrating higher than the old systems and old creations that still exist on the outside.

When we lose our current jobs, or when we simply cannot find employment anywhere, it is usually because we are being asked to dig deep within ourselves and to find out who we are and what we are here to contribute. We are literally being booted out of one reality and into another, whether we are seemingly ready or not! The new reality requires that we know who we are, why we are here, and what we are here to contribute, thus placing us in alignment with our true authentic selves and with Source.

In the year 2000, I could not get a job anywhere. I had been very blessed most of my life to easily get the jobs I had applied for, but suddenly, absolutely nothing was manifesting. I had hit a brick wall. Being a responsible person, I began to feel very uncomfortable. I was not willing to sit around and do nothing while I could not pay my rent or even buy food. I had been going through quite a transition during that time, was beginning to connect to some new and higher frequencies, and this was the result!

I thus began a deep process of soul searching and decided that I needed something that was really a good fit for me in all ways. I was finally able to get a job running the United Way in my area, but at that point I could no longer push, uplift, hold up, motivate, or make anything else happen, so I quit after just one day. I needed something that seemed effortless, was fun, and allowed me to utilize many of my interests, gifts, and talents. Very soon, the arena of grant writing popped up and was validated by some very big "signs" and away I went. Little by little, piece by piece, things miraculously fell into my lap. But then very shortly after, I crushed my leg and was catapulted into yet another massive transition. Again, wanting to be responsible, I thought I would resume grant writing work while on crutches. I was adamantly told "NO!" by the universe, and this time I listened. So from that point on, I never had a job again and have survived for over eight years with no real employment.

While in the long recovery process with my leg, I also began the intense process of ascension. It was then that I tried out many different creative modalities that I thought I would be interested in...some fit and some did not. It was then that I also had six months of traditional counseling, which greatly helped in cementing in who I really and truly was. Whenever I attempted to make any money through one of my new creative outlets, I would end up with a thriving business in only a week or two! If ever I became stressed and came from a stance that I *had* to make money from my creativity, nothing much would happen. But when I relaxed, enjoyed what I was doing, and did not care if it produced any income, I would get clients galore without any trying. It was then that I also began writing the energy alerts which fit me to a tee, and which I have now been writing for nearly seven years.

During that time, I also realized I did not want a business, did not want any rigid system of earning a certain amount of money for a certain measure of work, and really only wanted to relax, enjoy myself, and *be*. This is how I survive today in regard to money. I do not charge for my articles, or rather energy alerts, but simply love writing them and do not care much about how the money arrives. I do charge for books, but this is because I work with a publisher who needs a set way of doing business, and because to receive books in print, there are overhead costs to me met by others and not just me (the old reality). I make far more money from voluntary payments than from required payments. Mostly, I just love the writing and focus on that.

So how did I survive the process of "finding myself" and my new creative outlets without any money coming in? Who paid the bills when I could not get a job? And how did I get where I am today?

If we are at a point where we are uncomfortable with our current job situation, but have not been officially "released" by the universe (as I was when I was still able to get a job with United Way), then we are still at a point where we can create money generating work that fits us better while we are still in the old reality or mainstream. We can thus remain in the old reality while we create work that is more in alignment with where we are currently vibrating. In this way, we can continue to "tweak" a job description into one that may fit us better, as we have now evolved. We can make changes by becoming a consultant, for instance, that would allow us to remain out of the old world more. Or we can find new ways in which to express our gifts and talents that give us more freedom of choice, schedule, or the like. Or we can even do something different with our old job descriptions. There are many options available. The important ingredient is that we create "work" that fits the new us and our new desires in as many ways possible. We are then in alignment with where we are.

When we are in this space, we are then able to continue on a bit longer until we reach a place where we *must* make drastic changes. When we arrive at a point where we must make changes, it is because our soul plan is ready to be implemented, the time is now, and we must get on board. Our vibration is now simply too high for anything else. This is when our old job dramatically kicks us out, and we simply cannot get hired anywhere else. When this occurs, we are usually supported by the universe in strange ways until we can get up and going again...going again completely within our new arena and while very much in alignment with the new us and the new creations that we are now ready to give to the world.

When we are literally unable to work, even though we may try and are willing, it is because we are being given an opportunity to go to another level. *It is now time,* and our souls and the universe are setting everything up. We are being granted this opportunity and are being given this gift, or it would not be happening for us at all. If we can choose to surrender, let go, and accept this gift, then we will most assuredly be taken care of. We have to come to a point where we know with certainly that we are being lovingly watched over and everything will be OK. This takes a fair amount of trust. But once we surrender, everything will simply fall into our laps.

And this is what happened for me. Little by little, weird things would happen and I would receive money, either through the insurance company or through some other portal. In addition, the person who was driving the vehicle that I was a passenger in when I crushed my leg, felt badly and sent me some money every month as well. My attorney said he had never seen this happen before...he was quite amazed. I also had to get to a point where I was very willing to receive for doing nothing in return, and thus, get over the feelings I had that I was being irresponsible.

So then, eventually I was able to earn "money" doing what I loved, by simply being me, only "working" a few hours per week, and having absolutely no schedule, agendas, or responsibilities, thus fitting very nicely into the new reality which I was now a match for. It could be no other way. Through this seemingly stressful and dramatic process, I also came to know that I would *always* be taken care of. I knew that I had "earned" it through the ascension process, and that I would forever more be fine financially, and I have. I had reached the end of a road....all the "work" that I had done for the planet over the many years of my life (through the vehicle of me), was finally ready to manifest in abundance. And this is how I know it will for you as well.

When things slow down for me within my money generating portal, I simply do not care. Somewhere very deep I know that I am right where I need to be and will never go through financial struggle ever again. It is not worth the stress. I would rather leave this world than struggle again the way I did the first 46 years of my life. I do not care if my books sell, if my writing dries up, or much of anything else. It simply does not matter, and ironically, this is when everything arrives effortlessly. (But I *do* care if I am on track with my soul's direction...most certainly. This matters to me above all else.)

If you are one who has suddenly lost your stream of income, cannot find work even when you try, I would suggest to you that it is now time for your soul plan to kick in. The planet is now ready for your new and special contribution and the universe is simply giving you time to find it and to connect to it. If you are one who is very out of alignment with your current job situation, but you are still there, I would suggest to you that perhaps the planetary vibration is not quite ready for your ultimate soul contribution. You simply need to tweak or fine tune your current occupation into one that fits where you are vibrating right now. This does not mean that you are "behind" any others either. It can simply mean that you have been holding a particular space for the planet for a particular reason...all voluntary at your soul level. It may not be time yet for your ultimate soul contribution. We are always right where we need to be.

To confuse you even more, there are of course, always exceptions to these basic scenarios. If you are one who has a history of irresponsibility, of being a victim, or perhaps continuous experiences for many years of losing jobs or being out in the street, then you probably have some energies within you that you have not yet cleared or balanced. It can be easy at times to attribute all of our dilemmas to the ascension process, without looking closely within ourselves, but ascension is not always the culprit. The ascension process was not designed for us to suddenly be homeless and living out on the street. When we go through these at times dramatic changes, we are always taken care of if they are indeed caused by the ascension process. If you have been homeless for a long period of time, there is probably a very different cause for this, and it has nothing to do with the ascension process.

So then, we are still talking about money here. We are still talking about surviving *with* money. Until we progress to a state where we no longer need money, we will still need it for some things. Where are we ultimately headed, and how will we survive *without* money?

My soul memories of the end of the road look like this, but there is always room for change and different choices....this is the beauty of creation, as we are the ultimate creators:

Small communities will form in various areas of high vibration. These geographical areas will vibrate higher because they have either experienced a cleansing, or new energy has been released from beneath the Earth. The inhabitants of these areas will very naturally be drawn there for reasons of similarity of purpose. In other words, the vibration of the residents will match the vibration of the area. Each resident will contribute his or her own special passion, gift, or talent, there-by creating a piece of the whole. The center, or theme of the whole, will be the same for all inhabitants, but each contribution will be very different. In this way, all needs will be met by the passion or gift of another. The earth will also serve to provide what is needed. The earth possesses much, and all that is needed is to live in harmony with her as her bounty is utilized. She loves to provide! The celestial bodies will contribute as well, as the sun, moon, and planets have much to offer. In this way, all needs will be met without the need for money.

Several years ago I had some acquaintances who were very angry that the land in their area was being utilized for oil and gas. They protested frequently, became very hostile, and wanted to stop any excavation of gas and oil from the earth. They wanted to protect the earth. After hearing about this from them for a while, I finally decided to simply ask the earth how she felt about it. She very easily responded, "I don't mind at all that my bounty is being utilized. I love to share. It is the fighting and the way it is being distributed that is causing the problems."

Currently, I have living in my home a small community of spiders (well, it's not really a community....just a few). They are allowed to stay in my windowsills if they continue to catch flies. But they must stay in the windowsills, not run loose, and they must catch the flies...and they do. For a while, as you may remember, I had some rattlesnakes (not in the house!). They took care of the many gophers when they were here, but eventually I decided to have a talk with them as for various reasons I decided that they needed to reside further away from my house. I found that I truly liked rattlesnake energy after I connected with them. They are very laid back and easy going. But then the gophers came back! Eventually, a wonderful and quite large gopher snake arrived, and harmony was again restored.

There is a balance in all things, as most of us know. Here in New Mexico, it can be as harsh as it is beautiful. It is tough country, and at 7,000 feet, it can greatly help to be in harmony with nature. Many visitors who come here to live, have a mentality that they have to be tough...that they have to conquer the elements. They almost seem to take pride in their new toughness. But the Zuni have lived here for a very long time. They are soft spoken, gentle, open, accepting, and very easy. They do not conquer the elements and this land. They live in gentle harmony with it.

And this is how it will be with the communities, with the earth, and with the cosmos. An easy interaction of acceptance, reverence for the gifts of each contributor, seeing and honoring one another, and a beauty, peace, and ease with it all.

Until we are at this place with our evolutionary process, we will still need money. But as the ascension process unfolds in slow and steady steps, we will come to know that we continually have one foot in one reality and one foot in another. As we may eventually find ourselves living in pseudo communities, removed from the old reality, and having many of our needs met within them, we will still need money for some things for a while. In this way, money needs to know where to find us. It needs a portal or opening to come through. Thus, the store-fronts will arise.

Setting Up Our Store-Fronts

Our store-fronts will exist on the dimensional border so that they we will be poised to assist those who are yet to come where we are now. Others who are on their way need to be reached, and since they are not yet ready for "the other side," the dimensional border is a good halfway point...about as far as many of us who have been on their paths for a very long time , are able to travel and exist even for brief periods of time.

But like anything to do with the ascension process, there are many levels possible in regard to store-fronts before actually arriving on the dimensional border. Having a store-front set up on the dimensional border is indicative that one is ready and poised to offer their divine purpose to humanity. But until then, there are other levels of store-fronts which can exist much more in the old world, and not on the "dimensional border." As one progresses with his or her spiritual evolutionary process, he or she is less and less able to exist in the old world, but until he/she can absolutely exist there no more, having a store-front or portal for receiving money that is nearly completely within the old world, is still a viable option.

One way to continue to create money while still wholly enmeshed within the old reality, is to focus on service and humanitarian related endeavors. One can still make money in these pursuits and thus be in a bit of a higher vibrating energy while still existing within lower vibrating energies. So then, focusing on humanitarian issues and being in that space can greatly help. One rung lower would be to continue to create money by using your gifts and talents entirely within the old reality and within its systems, but to provide service to humanity as well while not necesarily making money from it.

Angelina Jolie, Tiger Woods, Michael J. Fox, Bill Gates, Jon Bon Jovi, Bono, and Oprah Winfrey are a few individuals who make their money by using their gifts, but they only utilize their money making arenas to sustain themselves so that they can do what they really and truly love the most....which does not necessarily create money. Their money making arenas also serve to sustain their higher passions, or rather their services to humanity.

Tiger Woods has said that golf pales in comparison to how he feels when he is involved with his new school. And Michael J. Fox has said that he never really came fully alive until he began his service work for Parkinson's Disease and stem cell research. Oprah Winfrey has created a school for girls in Africa, something she has wanted to do her entire life, and other outlets like her television show, keep her afloat and support these other endeavors, so that she is able to do what she really and truly loves.

So in this way, we can have a full and thriving store-front within the old reality that simply enables us to do what we hold most dear to our hearts. We need not, then, necessarily create money from what we love the most, or where our interests and desires are now taking us.

Let's go up another rung or two on the ascension ladder. Perhaps you are now unable to be around the old world much, but are still fairly comfortable being there *some* of the time. As mentioned before, you would then be able to consult, work from home, have more flexible hours, or anything else that would bring your occupation or area of expertise into a more highly vibrating space; a new space that matches where you are currently residing in the vibrational hierarchies. In this way, you are slowly exiting the old world, but can still stay afloat.

Your store-front would now be much more of who you are...you could express yourself much more clearly, easily, and in this way, more of the pure gold nugget of your authentic self would be available much more of the time. A purer energy of you would now be available without all the extras that really did not fit you in all ways. You could then choose what you wish to offer...the best of your purest and most inspirational of interests, and what you were truly good at while you were at your old job (i.e. only the aspects of it that you really liked doing). Being out of an office or group environment, or no longer working for someone else means that there would be less of the agendas, rules, structures, and boxes to fit into that exist for the old world and that do not always fit for each and every one who must live within them. We will eventually be residing and working together in groups as described earlier, but until they are vibrating high enough, we may need to stay in our current occupations, but in an individual way until we move up the ladder a few more rungs.

You now have more flexibility and can be more of you, so you may be happier and more content for a while.....but suddenly what you are interacting with no longer fits....as you have evolved once again. The way that things are accomplished within the old world and within the old systems has become intolerable for you now. It seems to make absolutely no sense to you, and you can take it no longer. You may not even like what you are offering anymore. And there may be a lower vibrating element that seems to have taken over as well...slowly infiltrating your old stomping grounds...increasing in numbers and authority, and you may begin to feel pushed out entirely from your old occupation.

So now what? Are you left hanging out there to dry? What in the world are you going to do? You have left your old job, cannot go back, and now your clients are drying up as well. As you are vibrating even higher now than your surroundings, things no longer seem to fit... and they certainly do not feel remotely good to be around. How are you going to survive when everything seems to be in some other place than where *you* are?

It is time for yet one more step up the evolutionary ladder. This is one of the more difficult steps because although it will place you in a much higher vibrating space and bring you much closer to "the other side," it takes a lot of courage and trust. But eventually, you will feel much better and feel much more at home with a renewed sense of place.

Before you take the next step, you may think that your time is over, that you have died, and that perhaps no one even knows that you exist. You may feel disconnected, alone, and totally helpless. You may begin to suddenly and strangely cling onto others, crave a bandwagon to jump onto, feel that you want to go to some place that has already been created, and just give up entirely. You may want to go where you know things are working, but where is that? Where is anything that is still functioning in a way that makes you feel at home and that you can relate to? Is anything up and running yet? Where are you supposed to go now? Is there anything left to hold onto?

It is now time to hold onto *you* and to a renewed and deeper connection to Source.

During this time, it can greatly help to know that you are simply going through the ascension process, like many, many others out there. You are not alone. Everyone is going with you, even though it may not seem like it. When we feel alone and lost, this is when our faith and trust can be utilized. The ascension process was not planned to leave us alone and helpless. Believe it or not, it was designed so that we could "ascend," or evolve and expand in the easiest way possible while still in human form. If you are the one you need to hold onto now, then you need to know who that "you" is.

You would not be in this situation if it were not time for this next step. Your soul is navigating the waters now, and will miraculously show you the way. Your soul is your partner, your best supporter, and the one who loves you the most. Strengthening your connection to your soul and to Source is now your next step. It is now time for you to do a self-excavating search and re-evaluation. You are being given an opportunity to dig deep, find out who you really and truly are, and why you are here at this particular time.

Releasing much of the old now places you in the new. So then, your store-front may now be very different from any of your store-fronts of the past. Now you get to bring forth what you have always wanted to bring forth. The pure gold nugget of you is now ready to be birthed and shared with the world. It is being given to you on a silver platter and you need only connect to it. It has been waiting for you all this time...for this very moment. You have arrived indeed.

You have found yourself in a space that is totally removed from the old world and old reality. Communities in your new space have not yet formed. Thus, you still have to survive on your own until more of the fall has taken place. The fall will rapidly encourage the formation of the new communities. All in divine and perfect order. With so much falling, unity will be paramount...and so will new beginnings.

"I'm much too stressed and scared to find out who I am right now!" you may be exclaiming. But this is where trust comes in. And you may be so weary of the whole process that you finally agree to let go, surrender, and allow your soul to come riding in on a white horse. It is now time for you to let go of the old. You do not live there anymore. You are in a new and different world now, and all your needs will be met if you allow this to be so.

So then, what are you good at? What will you be called to do? What can you simply not do? What interest and passion has been with you the longest? How can you assist humanity to the next rung of the evolutionary ladder? Will you heal those who are requesting healing in order to rise to the next level? Will you bring people up through a work of art or through music? Will you focus on our animal companions? What brings you the most joy? What would you do if you did not have to do anything else?

The store-fronts are designed to bring in income on the dimensional border while we are residing on the other side. When it is truly time in all ways after 2012, we will then be more focused on bringing forth our visions and talents for creating the very New World. These gifts, talents, and contributions for creating the New World may be the same as our store-fronts, or they may be completely different. And know as well, that our visions for the New World via our special contributions will begin when it is time...it does not necessarily have to be after 2012, as you may be a fore-runner. We can begin them now while at the same time providing our service to humanity in another reality. So then, new community contributions will most likely be about our creative outlets and not so much about serving humanity.

When we are serving humanity, we must go down a rung of the evolutionary ladder...or in other words, to a lower vibration. This is because the very things which are calling us to serve and assist with cannot possibly exist in the higher realms. In this way, we can stay in the lower vibrations without being totally clobbered, thrown off base, drained, or the like, if we remain focused and in the energy of love as well as the energy of our soul purpose. These two energies can keep us very connected to the higher realms and to Source until we are able to return to our sanctuaries where higher vibrating realities exist.

What will be your store-front? What is your calling? What we will offer to humanity will in itself keep us in a higher vibration because it is in alignment with us...it is our calling and part of our soul purpose. Our store-fronts are usually what we are very good at. Our store-front is usually something that comes very naturally to us. We are so good at it, in fact, that it is effortless. It fits us to a tee. We do not have to struggle with it, learn a lot about it, or "use notes" when we utilize it. We do it so effortlessly, that we may not even be aware that we are good at it. We just assume that everyone has this ability and talent because it has been with us for so long.

As there are many levels of store-fronts, we eventually find ourselves at a specific level that comes from a very deep place inside of us. As more and more of the denser and lower vibrating aspects of ourselves begin to drop away, we may also find that our needs seem to be miraculously met at each and every turn. It is then that we develop an overwhelming desire to serve humanity. Our store-fronts then become much more about service to the whole than about sustaining ourselves. And this is when we find that we can only provide a store-front which exists on the dimensional border, as we are now residing on the other side.

Knowing Our Path of Service

As we progress ever forward on our spiritual evolutionary journey, our thoughts and focus are directed less and less on ourselves and more onto what surrounds us. We are thus becoming more of a whole, as we come to know that we are all one and that what we do affects each and every part of that whole. Almost all of those bearing more light than most, experienced challenges of abuse and darker and denser energies when they were young. These challenges transpired so that light-bearers would be given the opportunity to transmute that darkness through themselves, there-by assisting all of humanity in the process. These experiences of darkness also served to encourage a summoning, searching, and desire for something better, and thus this questioning and yearning created the connection and remembrance of who we really were and why we were here at this particular time.

Very typically, experiences of abuse create a very self-absorbed individual. So then, getting out of ourselves, or our ego-selves was an even greater challenge. But the more we progress through the ascension process, the more we lose these ego-based aspects of ourselves, and the more we then connect to Source and our true authentic selves.

Everything is not about *us*. The more dense our energy is, or rather the more we embody lower vibrating energies within us, the more of a filter we see things through. Some call this ego, some may call this our mis-perceptions, and some may simply refer to this density as opinions. But as we progress spiritually, we begin to take things much less personally, as our filters or densities are dissipating. With more of our filters now out of the way, we begin to see that what we may be experiencing has less to do with us and much more to do with what is outside of us.

With much more of our old selves out of the way, any agendas we may have had are dissipated as well. As we progress spiritually, we being to possess a new agenda, and this new agenda does not derive from our lower vibrating ego selves. But know as well, that any agendas we may have are always a good fit for where we currently are. In this way, there is no right or wrong, or better or worse.

As we continue to progress spiritually, we also begin a knowingness and new experience of having all our needs met effortlessly, as we are then in a very new evolutionary space. It is then that we desire different things. It is then that we desire things relating to the whole. And it is then that we become more focused on utilizing our gifts to provide our service to humanity.

In our early stages of growth, we may find new and exciting ways of working with energy. We may learn about what the core of creating is about. We may suddenly have experiences of connecting with non-physical beings and the non-physical world. As we expand our consciousness and begin interacting with a higher vibrating reality, we may think that we have come far and are perhaps now "advanced" beings indeed.

But until we mature into these new ways of being, use them with wisdom and discernment, and utilize them in the ways in which they were intended, we are only playing with fire. Similar to creating an off-shoot of a refined and pure religion and warping it to the extent that it now does not remotely resemble its original purpose, mis-using energy, or running it through a very dis-connected filter, reflects a still dis-connected soul. This situation usually occurs when we jump too fast...when we do not fully embody a new energy within ourselves before we try to begin a new way.

Maturing gradually into a being that uses his or her gifts and talents wisely is paramount in regard to knowing our path of service. Our path of service almost always *calls to us*...we do not call to it. As we evolve, we find that we no longer decide what *we* want to do and then try and make it happen. When we arrive at a place where it is time to focus more intently on our path of service, it will arrive for us very naturally and it is usually not even our idea. It will most certainly arrive when we are ready and when we need not learn any more about our particular contribution, as we are now embodying it fully. If we have come to a place where we are simply happy within our passion, this is usually when we are called. We will then begin a process of preparation within ourselves....either through a cleansing, through losses (within and without), and the like. This is a holy moment. We are being called.

Thus, as we progress with our spiritual evolutionary process, we become less and less concerned with creating for our own self-interests, and more and more concerned with using our new awareness to create for the whole.

One of the many symptoms of ascension is finding ourselves talking and wondering who is doing the talking. It may seem that a voice is emanating from within us, but we may feel far removed from that voice. We may look in the mirror and not be aware of that particular self anymore. Becoming less and less aware of ourselves means that we have lost more and more of our old selves and are now much more connected to Source. We have now gotten out of our own way. And it is then that we begin to be more aware of what is outside of us than who we are and what is inside of us. Service to humanity is then the next natural stepping stone on our path of ascension.

We are now well on our way to becoming human angels of the earth. When we arrive at this space, we are here for several reasons. We are here because we have learned how to let go of compassion and move into love. We now know that we cannot and should not hold anyone up, fix things for anyone, and care so deeply that our energy drops into their space of pain and we are now where they are. We now know that we need only love them. Love them, revere them, and give them the due respect that all living creatures deserve. We are here now because we now know how to allow suffering to occur. We know that this is a natural process in the lower dimensions. We know now that suffering is an individual journey that serves to connect those who suffer more fully to Source. We know now that we need not save anyone from his or her own individual and holy journey. We know now that we need to be asked for our assistance, our wisdom, and our new knowledge, gifts, and talents. We know

now that we do not meddle, attempt to alleviate and fix, without each recipient of our services first coming to a point where he or she is ready...and when one is ready, one will ask.

And when they ask, a portal or door will open to the other side; another side where we are now residing and where we are willing and ready to assist others in joining us. Have you experienced pain and stiffness in your neck and back over the years and recent months? Have you had an aching and pain that could not be explained in these areas? Our angel wings are attempting to sprout. They are readying to burst forth, open through the density of our old human bodies, and serve to carry us in a cloud of light as we serve humanity. We are becoming human angels of the earth indeed.

As we become much more aware of what surrounds us the more we get out of our own way, we begin to know that there are others out there who are not residing on this planet, but who are none-the-less very connected to us as well. The higher we begin to vibrate or to evolve, the more ease we will have in connecting with these non-physical beings. I frequently refer to them as the Star Beings.

Connecting With the Star Beings

A rule of energy states that we connect with energies that are vibrating where we are vibrating. Thus, when we are just beginning to open and expand, we may find ourselves connecting to just about anything in the non-physical world. But as we progress in our growth process, we find that we begin connecting to higher vibrating and much more advanced non-physical beings the more we advance ourselves.

At the lower levels of the dimensional hierarchies, it can be easy to connect to our deceased loved ones who are many times at the next dimensional level above us. If we can know how easily accessible they are to us, this can bring great relief and comfort during times of their parting.

When my grandmother passed away at age 97, I was not as prepared as I thought. Although we knew for awhile that she was on her way to the other side, at age 52, I still had never really experienced the loss of a loved one before. So then, when I received the news, I was grief stricken none-the-less. My grandmother and I had a special bond like no other. The following day I was in a restaurant having breakfast with a friend. Very suddenly, seemingly out of the blue, I burst into tears. Feeling uncomfortable in public in this state of being, I went out towards the car. While standing there, I felt a hand upon my shoulder...the hand of my grandmother. She proceeded to tell me that I was the strongest person she knew, and certainly within the entire family, and thus she knew I would be fine. And she was *so happy!* Each and every soul whom I have spoken with from the other side, usually at the request of a relative, is always so happy!

After that, I never experienced a sad moment again. And I cannot tell you how often I talk to my grandmother now. It is like she never left. She is with me always.

There are other dimensional levels and other realities that we can connect to as well. When I used to frequent the ancient sites here in the Southwest, I frequently spoke to the ancients who were no longer in physical form. Their energies were fairly easy to discern. The Mogollons, for instance, were a more pristine, innocent, pure, and original energy than the Anasazi who had succumbed to the lower vibrating energies of power and the like. I preferred connecting, then, to the more original and pristine ancients.

Many groups of ancients have touched the earth in times past. They arrived at different times and for various reasons. Being that I have spent the most time with the Mogollon culture, I grew then, to know more of their ways. They indeed lived in harmony with the earth and the cosmos. They indeed lived a very clean, clear, and pristine existence. They knew how to set up their communities in alignment with specific energies. They knew what to put where. They created illusion for unwanted visitors...this was their non-violent defense mechanism. They knew how to place grinding slicks in alignment with the equinox, solstice, and energies of the sun and moon. And they ground things dear to them, specific stones and the like, when the alignments were just so, in order to wear and utilize these aligned substances all the time. These are but a few of their ways...the ways that our present day culture has now forgotten.

My connection to the ancients was only meant to be brief. Although I enjoyed this time immensely, this was not my passion or area of expertise. Their ways of utilizing and living with alignments will always be a part of me, as this particular aspect of their culture remains to be utilized today. Alignments are very powerful indeed and can serve to ease our existence in many ways. So these ways, then, are what I will use when building my home here in New Mexico.

But ultimately, I was more comfortable speaking with the higher authority that sent the ancients here in the first place. He became a friend to me during these times. A gracious, calm, wise, and ancient being himself, we had many conversations. Ultimately, he released me to continue on somewhere else. Saying that I was always welcome at the sites, he encouraged me to simply visit them, commune with the inhabitants there, and to forgo learning anymore about their ways. I was simply to visit, have fun, enjoy, and relax.

We are now vibrating beyond the level of the ancients. We have surpassed them. Although there are always high vibrating things from the past to be brought forth into the future, we are meant to create fresh and new, the New Earth of our choosing.

Because of the plan of the Shift of the Ages, we are being given infinite choices as to what the New Earth will look like. It is entirely up to us, as we are the ones experiencing

Karen Bishop

the ascension process while in physical form on the earth, and we are then, the ultimate creators.

As each and every one of us participating in the Shift of the Ages is a representative from our home or star, we are thus very connected to our star families. And this brings us to another level and very interesting scenario relating to the Star Beings.

Some of our star families are more evolved and vibrate higher than others. A highly evolved being vibrates similarly to our new vibrations as the angels of the earth. So then, higher vibrating Star Beings will not tell you what to do, order you around, ask you to do something for them, or set up situations that benefit them and are detrimental to you. They will not meddle, give you unsolicited advice, arrive in your space uninvited, or the like.

I disconnected from my star family many years ago. I did not like the way I felt when they spoke to me, I felt I was being utilized by opportunists, and I felt they were unnecessarily harsh, rude, and disrespectful. There are some Star Beings that need to clear up damage that they incurred here on the earth in times past. And they want their offshoots or representatives to do this for them. They are trying to clear their energy so that they can move forward. They have a distinct agenda. I am sure there are other lower vibrating reasons for utilizing human beings as well, but I choose not to go there or even have this information in my space.

Other Star Beings are stuck in the past and have completely missed the boat. They do not seem to be aware that we are undergoing an ascension process, that we are creating a very new planet Earth, and they are thus trapped in a merry-go-round relating to their agendas from some lower vibrating reality. We tried to bring everyone together here for this Shift of the Ages, and at times things can unfold in a variety of ways indeed...but these are the old ways. Although they need to clear their energies before they can move on, it is best that they do it with a fully consenting and willing human being who is joyful about doing their bidding.

Those of us who experienced challenges and darker energies earlier in our lives as mentioned previously in this book, almost always have boundary issues. This is very common and to be expected...and this is yet another challenge of those bearing the most light. But if we have taken responsibility for our healing, chosen to look inside of ourselves and be brave enough to see what is there, and are willing to know and accept what healthy boundaries are all about, our process with any outside energies will be much more of a pleasant experience.

We will attract in the non-physical world the same things we attract in the physical world. So although we may think that we have evolved and expanded because we can now easily connect to the non-physical world, if we are not yet ready and healthy within, we will have some strange and unpleasant experiences indeed, and may not even be aware of what is occurring. This is why a stepping stone process is so vitally important; and this is also why the New Age community gets a well earned bad rap at times. Many have simply not yet matured into their area of interest and are thus, mis-managing, mis-handling, and utilizing their newfound knowledge in inappropriate and immature ways.

In regard to boundaries, it is not the best possible scenario to allow just anything into our spaces. We have a right to say "no." We need not be nice, or even believe or buy into what has arrived in our spaces just because it is of the non-physical world. It is *always best* to use our good judgment. If something does not feel good, right, or seems awry, we can simply say, "No thank you." My rule of thumb relates to assessing if I am being considered, respected, or empowered. Some might say that the non-physicals simply do not understand as they are not in human form, but I say that is a very lame excuse provided by a lower vibrating being.

So then, many times we are vibrating beyond our star families. We have outgrown them. And many times we are vibrating beyond many of the non-physical beings in which we come into contact. But this is perfectly OK and very natural for a very specific reason.

If one were to speak to Archangel Michael, for instance, one might receive a message in one form or another. Another individual might speak to Archangel Michael and receive yet another. In long times past, when I used to read the material of others, I was always amazed, for instance, at all the astrological references Archangel Michael made for one individual but not for another.

When we are communicating with and connecting to a non-physical being, we are actually connecting to an aspect of ourselves. So then, we are only speaking to ourselves. Most of us may not be ready to accept the higher vibrating, wise, and wonderful aspects of ourselves, so we subconsciously choose to place them outside of us. But we would not be connecting to them at all if they were not a part of us. We simply are not ready yet to accept the fact that we are incredibly awesome and wise, so we attribute these traits to another. Thus, in our lower vibrating 3D minds, we make up a story or a scenario that we can wrap our minds around, as this can at times, be easier to digest.

The ascension process and plan was described at the beginning of this book. And included within this description was the fact that we are all one...that we embodied each and every manifestation of energy at some point. Thus, we *are* the non-physical beings as well. As we begin to expand and grow, or to vibrate higher, we then surpass the aspects of ourselves that are vibrating lower. In this way, when we reach new plateaus of expansion, we almost always receive and connect to very new "guides" in the non-physical. These new guides are again, simply aspects of ourselves that we are now a better match for, and being that we place them outside of ourselves, can connect to with more ease, trust, and companionship.

The more we evolve, the less we depend upon information outside of us. A higher vibrating guide will usually disappear when we are in distress. This is because we are being encouraged to find our answers *within*. A higher vibrating guide does not want us to become dependent upon it. There have been many times in my life when I called out to my non-physical companion and he seemed to be behind an energetic wall. He would tell me that he was not "allowed" to come into my space. Although he seemed so very far away, I understood what was occurring, and ultimately was grateful for it.

In our beginning stages of spiritual evolution, we can greatly benefit from information from outside sources (as long as we do not become dependent upon them). In the same vein, we can also benefit from assists as well. Divination card decks, readings from those who can see what we may not, and most certainly advice from the non-physicals. In these cases, we are only being validated for what we already know at some level.

In regard to assists with our healing, they can be greatly beneficial in the beginning stages as well. Until we come to a point where we are vibrating high enough that we rarely become ill or out of balance, or when we have not yet reached a level where we know how to rebalance ourselves very naturally, assistance with healing and rebalancing can be very necessary and certainly helpful.

But once we evolve beyond these supports, connecting with them will only serve to bring us down into a lower vibrating space. You will know when you have reached this new plateau in your evolutionary process, as receiving a healing or adjustment will feel downright awful, and not because you are releasing. It will feel as if you are reactivating something that has been dormant and no longer fits you, it will feel very "off" or strange, it will feel dense and as if you have dropped lower somehow, and you will feel even more out of balance than when you began.

So then, I will say to you that the more we evolve, the less we connect to, speak with, and commune with the non-physical world in ways of the past. This is because we are becoming non-physical ourselves...we are becoming what it was that we used to depend upon in the past...we are becoming the angels of the earth. And ultimately, we will evolve beyond any and all non-physical beings in this universe. It is then that we will be ready to begin a brand new journey in a brand new and more highly vibrating universe where we have yet to travel.

After we begin to understand and become comfortable connecting with the Star Beings, we will find a new and higher vibrating relationship with them. We were meant to be the ultimate creators of this New Planet Earth. We were meant to create it in the ways of our choosing...not then, in the ways that some Star Beings are attempting to place upon us that existed in the old 3D reality. In this way, a highly vibrating Star Being will wait to be asked. They know that this is our game. They know that although we are aspects of them, we are the ones here in form at this time, experiencing this amazing and challenging ascension process. They know that we are evolving *for them* as well. And they know and remember the plan that says it is up to those of us who are here on the planet to choose what we will create.

What if you are one who has never connected to a Star Being or anything from the non-physical world? Is there something wrong with you? If you do not want to, you certainly don't have to, and thus, you probably won't. I have been this way since I was born, so this is the only way of being I have known in this lifetime. But what if you are ready and willing to begin a connection and you have not had an experience like this before?

This book was not intended to give a detailed lesson on connecting to the non-physical world, but I know there are assuredly many wonderful teachers and programs out there that can provide this service. For our purposes here, know that we all have this ability within us. All of us have a muscle that can be developed with practice and with use. If you are willing to begin a connection, all you need do is to be open and willing. Ask that a higher vibrating being show its' presence to you in a way that you will recognize. We are all different, and thus, we receive information and much of anything else in a way that is specific to us. In this way, some of us may hear, others may see, and yet others may simply sense. There is always the way of connecting through writing as well.

The angel community is a wonderful arena to start with. They always vibrate high and are a joy to communicate with.

When my new twin grandbabies were born prematurely in June of 2008, they were in the Neonatal Intensive Care Unit for many weeks. In a panic, my daughter asked that I dispatch some angels to watch over them, but this was not necessary. It was not necessary because when I looked into the hospital, there were wall to wall angels everywhere! I have never seen so many angels in one place at one time. It was a sight to behold and brought me to tears. Our angels are so incredibly loving, non-judgmental, always willing to serve, and so very gentle. I just love the angels!

As we begin living in communities that vibrate higher, a part of this way of living involves regular communication with the Star Beings. We are all one in this universe, and having an on-going connection and welcome mat with other life forms will be a normal part of our existence. The ancients lived in this way as well. They provided beacons at their sites for connecting and were very aware that they were not the only ones around.

Do we have to live in this way? What if each and every one of us has a different vision of a higher vibrating reality? Then what?

Finding Our Heaven

When we crossed over to the other side through the death process in the old 3D reality, we were given an opportunity to bask for a while in whatever illusion we chose. We could fish 24/7, eat bonbons all day, or perhaps simply lie in a field of wildflowers and pet our animal companions. And sometimes we needed a much deserved rest for a while so that we could rejuvenate before we started again. But eventually, having all our needs and dreams met with ease became boring (and yes at times we may have stayed in this state for too long and were then gently nudged by our guides to possibly get moving!).

Ultimately, we arrived in spaces where we desired opportunities to create and to serve. Creating is a mainstay for energy. And while in form, we always seek ways to create. At higher levels we created planets, solar systems, and then placed life within them; and at times, placed aspects of ourselves within them, just for fun and for a new experience. At other levels, we seek to create in different ways. We may choose to create a painting, a song, a garden, a written piece, or perhaps even a new home to live in. The higher we evolve, the more time we spend creating.

Our Heaven, then, can be whatever we want it to be. Many times we may think we know what we would like our immediate reality to look like, and then very suddenly we evolve beyond that vision and it no longer fits who and where we are. We may also envision something that we believe is a possibility, and not necessarily something that we really and truly desire.

As we progress ever so swiftly along our ascension paths, we may also discover that not much really matters. What we may have thought was so vitally important to us, now seems moot. When we go through and experience suffering or great loss, or perhaps witness the suffering and losses of our loved ones, we may soon find ourselves redefining what it is that is really and truly important to us....or in other words, what really and truly matters above all else.

So then, as we evolve and step upon new and different rungs of the ascension ladder, we have the opportunity to create whatever we choose at any given moment. And as our choices become more and more refined the more we release and purge what has been within us, our creations do as well. This is the fun of creating...it is forever on-going depending upon where we are, and as always, all in divine and perfect order.

Have you had a vision for a very long time that has never changed even when you may have changed? If everyone's needs were always met, including yours, and suffering no longer existed...if there was no longer a need for healing, what would you create? What would your reality look like? What would you do with yourself? What then, is your vision of Heaven on Earth?

The closer we come to living in our paradise, the more that two things seem to continually remain: *Service to humanity and the need to create.*

Living within our own sacred sanctuaries, whether they be our own special homes or our own special communities, can now give us the opportunity to provide our own special contribution through our own special creations. The more we evolve, the closer we will come to this scenario.

We innately want others there with us. We will then very naturally evolve into a life that consists of living in our sacred communities. There, all our needs will be met as we contribute to the whole through our own unique gifts, passions, and creations. The remainder of the time we will simply enjoy our brothers and sisters, enjoy ourselves, and enjoy the earth and cosmos that surrounds us. Until the rest of the planet is where we are, we will continue to offer our gifts of service to humanity...a humanity that exists in another world, but that is willing and ready to receive help, guidance, and the services that will assist them in moving up the evolutionary ladder.

Until then, we are able to create any reality and version of Heaven that we choose. It is entirely up to each and every individual on the planet what his or her Heaven on Earth will be. And we can stay in that reality as long as we choose.

~Staying In Our Heaven ~

Truth be said, reading this entire book is not really necessary. Although there are explanations within it, that may serve to validate and give an understanding of some of the processes of energy and evolution, and although it may serve as a guide on our journey, ultimately, we really do not need to know any of it.

As we eventually evolve into new and higher states of being, things become much simpler. We do not hold onto much, as we are simply in the moment, which places us in the center space of stillness. The only thing that is really and truly important is the now, as we can create fresh and new in any given moment.

We ultimately find that the trivial things in life are really not that important. Nothing needs to be as perfect as we think it should be. We truly come to know that simple beauty in all things....the smile of an infant, the hug of a child, the laughter of a loved one, the purring of a cat, the joyful running of a dog, an amazing sunset, the smell of the rain on a sagebrush mesa, or sitting in a bed of wildflowers are all things that exist right now.

Reading long texts and complicated books becomes more and more difficult, as we are now evolving higher and thus, are tired, cannot process too much, do not *need* to process too much, and are beginning to evolve ever more fully into the simplicity of simply *being*. As we learn to let go of much, only a few simple things are what truly matter...and nothing needs to be "fixed."

Thus, staying in our Heaven then becomes more about staying put, staying centered, and simply following our hearts while ignoring all the periphery, as it really has nothing to do with us anymore.

There is so much information out there these days, that one might become confused with all the differing opinions and stances. The more information that is put out there and considered in any given arena, the more confusing it can be. But as we evolve higher and higher, we come to know that opinions, information, and the like, always come from a filtered source. One seeming authority may tell us one thing, and another may tell us something completely different. The more density that remains within us, the more of a filter we will communicate and receive through. In this way, we could simply disregard any and all information that is flying around out there, as much of it is biased. Our higher selves, or our souls, can see things from a higher perspective. They do not need any information. They can see what is really and truly going on very easily. They reside above all the filters and opinions. They have a clear shot...they see through the density.

In regard to my energy alerts and my web site, I am not easily accessible to the outside world. I do not give out my e-mail address. One of the main reasons is because of all the varying opinions I would have to spend my time wading through. I would rather spend my time in my purpose. Within the correspondences I do receive, are a fair amount of these:

"I am tired of hearing all about you and your life. I am unsubscribing."
"I love your personal stories! Thank you so much for sharing yourself!"

"I am sick of everything always coming back to Phil. I won't read you anymore."

"What is going on with you and Phil? Why haven't we heard about him for awhile?"

"I am an astrologer and checked out Obama. He is terrible...a big phony who sucks the energy of his wife!"

"Please tell us more about the higher soul purpose of Obama. I need to feel safe and secure again. I know he is from the light. I am afraid and know others would like more higher level information about him."

"You are far too dark and negative. I am in a happy space and do not feel anything that you are describing. You need to go outside and take a walk and get out of the muck you are in."

"Thank you so much for validating where I am! I was so confused, but now I know why I was feeling this way, know that there was a higher purpose and reason, and now there is hope!"

"Don't you know that we are not supposed to be 'going' anywhere? It is all about being in the moment."

"Thank you so much for telling us what is going on and why. Now I know I am not 'going" insane, simply evolving and moving forward!"

Personal filters are the way most of us see things until we are vibrating high enough to see with the clarity that a higher dimensional residency provides.

One way to stay in our Heaven, then, is to remove ourselves from all the opinions out there. When we stay in our center, or stay put, we soon find that we need something to occupy ourselves with, as we are now out of the old reality of lower vibrating opinions and filters. And this is when our creativity and connection to ourselves and to Source become a very viable option.

We can stay in Heaven when we know who we are. We can stay in Heaven when we are so absorbed in our creative outlet, that this is where we place our attention. When we know who we are, and are aligned with it, while either in our creativity or providing our service and contribution to humanity, we are always connected.

Staying in this space, placing our time and attention there, and disregarding much of the outside energies, will very naturally place us in alignment with Heaven, and thus, we need not ever know or understand the why of anything. We are simply being. Just like the flower in nature, we know who we are and are simply being just that. The remainder of the time, we simply just get to have fun.

When we are in alignment with who we are, we can then stay centered and in our Heaven much more easily. In times past, we experienced higher energy shifts that arrived from solar flares, or from the "outside." We are now vibrating high enough that we can sustain ourselves. We have purged and refined so much of our internal energy, that we can now embody much more light within.

As we come to know who we really and truly are, while embodying much more of our pure authentic selves without all the periphery, we will then begin connecting more and more to each other. The light then, is coming much more from the inside than from the outside than in times past. Connecting many purified "lights" will indeed create a magnificent whole.

Staying in Heaven then, involves connecting to ourselves and eventually connecting to each other (after we rise above all the filters!). In the meantime, staying in our spaces of creativity and knowing what it is ours to do in service to the planet, will place us continually in a space of Heaven on Earth.

We need not know anything else, other than what is ours to do and be. Nothing else matters. Everything else then becomes trivial and inconsequential at best, or someone else's version of Heaven.

We can stay in our passion. We can stay in our creativity. We can stay in our own special gift to humanity. We can follow the path of where we feel good and where we truly feel like ourselves. And the remainder of the time, we simply get to have fun. It is then that we know we have arrived in Heaven on Earth.

About the Author

Karen Bishop is the creator of *What's Up On Planet Earth?*, a website devoted to our spiritual evolutionary process and living in the new energies. Recognized as an authority on ascension, Karen has reached thousands of readers worldwide through her weekly energy alerts about human and planetary evolution, and through her books since 2002.

A life-long clairvoyant, sensitive, multidimensional traveler and communicator, she has herself undergone the challenges and mysteries of the ascension process. With her background, training, and experience in soul purpose work, she continues to assist her readers in identifying their own unique gifts, talents, and special contribution to the world, as well as assisting others in integrating the new and higher ways of living with the new energies

With an educational background in psychology, counseling, and law, Karen has served as a facilitator, counselor, and teacher, working with county agencies, non-profit agencies,

Native American tribes, public school systems, and various individuals.

Currently residing in the mountains of New Mexico, she follows her joy and passion through writing, sewing, painting, enjoying time in nature, and experiencing the new energies and the non-physicals.

For more information about Karen and her latest messages and writings about spiritual evolution, living in the higher realms, and identifying your soul purpose, please visit her website at: http://whatsuponplanetearth.com. You may contact Karen through her website.

Printed in the United States
127324LV00002BA/88-576/P